BOLD. BLACK.
& BECOMING

A Psychology Guide to Heal & Thrive

DR. ABENA BERRY

Bold. Black. & Becoming
A Psychology Guide to Heal & Thrive

ISBN 979-8-9907826-0-0

Library of Congress Control Number: 2024910306

Published by:
Dr. Abena Berry
Illinois, USA

To my eternal soulmate, who continuously breathes life into me and encourages me to live to my full potential.

And to the living manifestation of our love, EJ, being your mother is the greatest purpose life has gifted me.

I love you both endlessly.

Contents

A Special Message to My Non-Black Readers

Thank you so much for choosing to read *Bold. Black. & Becoming* and for supporting a Black author! Since psychology applies to everyone, anybody, regardless of race or culture, can benefit from the mental health knowledge and tools I share in this book. Hopefully, you will learn a lot of valuable information that will be useful during the rest of your healing and growth journey.

Along with the mental health benefits, you will also increase your awareness of Black experiences, and it may shed light on your areas of privilege. Of course, we all face hardships and have some privileges, but many of us have more privileges than others due to multiple factors, including race. Someone else's pain does not invalidate our own, just as someone else's success doesn't mean our accomplishments are less significant. Our suffering should not be a source of competition but a source of empathy; we all deserve to be seen and validated.

Your decision to read this book shows that, in addition to caring about your mental health, you also care about understanding people who are different from you. I am so grateful for your willingness; when we empathize with each other, we create safe spaces for everyone. Our differences are some of the most beautiful parts of our humanity. However, we can only fully appreciate this when we live authentically, celebrate our uniqueness, and acknowledge each other's experiences. When we take the time to understand one another, we do less harm and deepen our human connections, ultimately making the world a better and more peaceful place for us all. Thank you so much for choosing to be part of this goal! ♥

A Special Message for All Who Choose to Read This Book

Before you begin, please read!

Before diving into *Bold. Black. & Becoming*, it's important to know that it must be approached the same way I recommend you approach your self-development: with an open, curious mind. You may find ideas in this book that challenge your current beliefs, and that's okay. It doesn't mean they have to change. That's entirely up to you! However, it is undeniable that having our beliefs challenged is an essential part of our personal development. After all, nothing changes if nothing changes.

I am by no means telling you what to believe; that's not my right. We are all humans with free will, and your beliefs are rightfully your own. I genuinely desire for you to form your own perspectives because I do not have all the answers. None of us do. I'm simply presenting scientific facts and sharing skills and tips to help you better manage your mental health while simultaneously giving you ideas to consider as you continue on your life's journey. Please feel free to disregard any part of this book you feel is unhelpful to you. I hope you get tremendous value from it overall. Happy reading, friend! ❤

Introduction:
Where's Your Superhero?

I n fictional stories, there's a familiar narrative in which superheroes rescue innocent people by defeating the villain. Although often done creatively, this storyline has been told countless times. Yet, we continue to feel a sense of satisfaction from a story that begins with devastating chaos and unfolds seamlessly into a happy ending. We love seeing the hero save the day because it represents what we all want: to be rescued from our problems and live *happily ever after*.

I once was one of those innocent people waiting to be rescued. As we all did, I entered the world as an excited baby full of life and potential. Unfortunately, I was confronted by many "villains" during my journey to adulthood. For me, those villains came in various forms, including generational trauma, sexual predators, school bullies, and psychologically abusive relationships. These experiences were life-altering, and even as a child, I fantasized about the person who would rescue me.

For a long time, I believed all I had to do was find someone who would wash away all the pain from my past. But as I got older, I realized the movies got it wrong. Life isn't that simple. It was up to me to rescue myself by seeking help, unlearning what I needed to unlearn, and taking accountability for my healing (despite not being responsible for my trauma).

The truth for all of us is that we are both the innocent person who needs rescuing and the superhero capable of and responsible for doing it. The person coming to save you is the version of you that *chooses* to be dedicated to doing healing self-work. You must become that person to be saved.

Don't get me wrong. Other people have played, and still play, a significant role in my growth. Nevertheless, they can only have that impact on my life because I *allow* them to. Other people play an essential role in our mental healing, but their support is only as valuable as we allow. Furthermore, it is up to us to seek guidance and support from the *right* people and sources. This makes all the difference because, just like the superheroes in movies, our battles are most easily won with help. Someone else can educate you, show you healthier behaviors, teach you new skills, positively challenge you, and even protect you. Still, ultimately, it's up to *you* to benefit from that help. As the saying goes, "You can lead a horse to water, but you can't make it drink."

One of our greatest challenges is acknowledging the unintentional role we've played in preventing our healing. We also have to accept how we have caused ourselves preventable distress through our choices. Maybe we were offered healthy help and guidance, but for one reason or another, we were not in a mental space where we could sincerely receive it. Whether due to pride or a fear of change, we all, at one time or another, have unintentionally contributed to our distress by not doing what's best for us.

Despite being responsible for these choices, *we must not crucify ourselves* because they aren't inherently our fault. Most of these choices are behavior and thought patterns we can trace back to our unresolved traumas. Suppose a person grows up in a home witnessing a toxic, unhealthy marriage. Due to conditioning, over time, that experience subconsciously becomes "normal" for them, putting them at a significantly higher risk of ending up in a similar situation. After all, our parents' interactions with one another and with us are our first and primary examples of relationships. These interactions set the tone for how we display affection (or not), how we express emotions, and what relationship behaviors we consider acceptable or typical.

Our parents influence our attachment style, the distinctive way we behave in intimate relationships, and our internal narrative (i.e., what we think about ourselves and our experiences). These and other events during our upbringing influence our behaviors, self-image, and worldview.

Research has repeatedly shown that in the case of *unhealthy, unhappy marriages,* divorce tends to be *significantly healthier* for all parties (i.e., the parents and children) since remaining in the union often causes severe emotional, psychological, and behavioral problems for everyone involved. Think of it this way. As you were growing up, if your parents had told you the color blue was called red, you would have believed them. As children, we are vulnerable because we have no frame of reference besides what our parents teach us through their words, but most importantly, their actions.

Yet, crucifying our parents (or anyone else) is not the way to go because it isn't the best use of our emotional energy. Plus, doing so won't lead to our healing. Our parents' behaviors resulted from their unresolved trauma, a cycle known as generational trauma because it's passed down from generation to generation until someone chooses to seek healing. We shouldn't punish our parents, but we should *always* hold people accountable for how they have hurt or failed us (even if they had the best intentions). Someone's unresolved trauma is an *explanation* for their behavior toward us, but not an *excuse* for those behaviors. Holding people accountable allows us to acknowledge our experiences for what they were. It helps us gain a deeper understanding of what we went through and the impact it had on us, which is essential for our healing and ending the cycle of trauma.

If we minimize what we went through and its impact on us, we invalidate our own experiences and deprive ourselves of the ability to recover from them. After all, we can't heal wounds we refuse to acknowledge, and we must dig deep to see how far the damage goes to heal it properly. Minimizing or ignoring it doesn't allow for either.

If you want to break generational curses and heal, you must first learn to see yourself as a superhero capable of doing so. The fact that you're reading this book means you either already believe in your capabilities or, at the very least, are open to the possibility. If you are struggling, please know I wrote this book because I wholeheartedly believe in you! It's my way of providing tools to help you strengthen your belief that *you are a capable superhero.*

As you read and digest *Bold. Black. & Becoming,* you will learn a wide range of mental health knowledge, including the following information:

- How psychology—the science of the human mind, emotion, and behavior—helps us deeply understand ourselves and others
- How psychology explains the *"why"* behind what we do, how we think, and who we are
- Common pitfalls of your thought patterns and how they relate to your behaviors
- A bit about the impact racism, stereotyping, and oppression have on the Black psyche
- The relationship between your thoughts, emotions, and behaviors
- A healthier perspective of life that creates feelings of empowerment and improves decision-making
- The power of adopting a mindset that highlights your free will and freedom of choice

- How you can use psychology to help yourself and other human beings
- Insight regarding how your trauma *may* have affected you

In short, *Bold. Black. & Becoming* aims to give you psychological knowledge and tools to help you figure out how to save yourself. The information presented here will by no means be everything you need to heal and evolve. However, my deepest hope is that it will be a valuable part of your growth journey as you continue to seek all the resources you need. Remember: a crucial part of being a superhero is receiving help from multiple sources. Please know some people want to help you achieve your goals. Whether through therapy with a trained professional, finding

> This book *cannot* account for every reader's life story and does not attempt to do so. Individual trauma-focused therapy with a licensed professional is the best way to learn how your specific trauma experiences have affected you. The information in this book is based on *general* psychology only.

mentors in your life, watching educational videos, or reading more self-help books, other people (the right people) can provide you with the tools you need to rescue yourself.

If you've already begun your healing work, I hope you can take lessons from this book to further your growth. If you haven't started yet, I hope this book inspires you to begin engaging in self-work. Yes, it is frustrating that you did not ask to be traumatized but are then responsible for addressing the impact your trauma had on you. It's undeniably unfair that the trauma you didn't ask for burdens you with the massive responsibility of healing from it. You came into the world relying on adults to teach and model the right things. Problematically, many of these adults were failed by their caregivers during their upbringing and never did the necessary work to begin healing. Despite their love for you, they went on to fail you too. But if you don't take responsibility for your healing, you continue to suffer, and this cycle will cause you to do the same to the people you love.

I am immensely sorry for the experiences that have negatively impacted your well-being up to this point. I also want you to know they don't have to continue to control your life's narrative. They don't have to determine how your story ends. Your future is unwritten, and only you decide on the next chapters. There are no shortcuts to healing or personal growth; it is a lifestyle and lifelong commitment that takes dedication and hard work. But out of everything you could commit to, doing all you can in this lifetime to continuously evolve into better versions of yourself is the most valuable, and it benefits everyone with whom you come in contact.

You deserve to have the life you want.
You deserve to heal from your trauma.
You deserve to know yourself deeply.
You deserve to meet and live as your authentic self.
And you deserve to be saved by a superhero.

CHAPTER 1

Why You Should Care & How Psychology Can Help

You are the greatest project you will ever work on, and the work continues for a lifetime.

B eing Black in America (and most parts of the world) comes with its challenges. Our struggles start with judgments based on the color of our skin and are further fueled by people's ignorance, stereotypes, and hate. Despite how hard the world has historically tried to make it to love ourselves, we continue celebrating our light-to-dark skin tones, unique cultures, beautiful Black features, and creativity. We have achieved impressive levels of success and continue to evolve as a highly diverse and culturally rich group of people.

Despite all our outstanding accomplishments, it is also important to acknowledge that not all of us have been able to thrive. Statistical data shows we experience certain traumas at a higher rate than other racial groups:

- Black people have the highest rate of post-traumatic stress disorder (PTSD).[1]
- In the past two decades, suicide rates for Black males 10-19 years old have increased by 60%.[2]
- The adult Black community is more likely to have chronic feelings of sadness, hopelessness, and worthlessness.[3]
- Rates of mental health conditions continue to rise within Black communities.[4]
- The adult Black community is 20% more likely to experience serious mental health problems, such as Major Depressive Disorder or Generalized Anxiety Disorder.[5]

Of course, these experiences are not unique to Black people. They occur for humans across the board. However, when viewed from a trauma lens, it is undeniable that our Blackness gives us a unique lived experience, and these statistics are very concerning.

To put it plainly, being Black in the world we currently live in is traumatizing. Things are improving, but we are still far from peace and equity. The trauma statistics for Black people are heartbreaking. We're exposed to hate crimes and prejudice through our personal experiences and the media. We constantly jump hurdles, like navigating implicit biases and microaggressions. We are also still psychologically recovering from the adverse effects of slavery and segregation.[6]

To make matters worse, harmful stigmas and misinformation regarding mental health plague Black communities.[7] These beliefs have prevented many of us from understanding the value of mental health treatment. Plus, certain societal barriers, such as disparities in healthcare coverage, make pursuing treatment challenging.[8] Despite a steady increase, there is still a shortage of Black therapists, which discourages many Black people from getting the help they need.[9] All these factors and more have deprived us of knowledge that can help us better understand ourselves emotionally, psychologically, and behaviorally. The consequences of this incomprehension have been dire for many due to trauma's severe impact on their psyche.

Scientifically, we have long known that traumatic experiences negatively impact our brains and bodies. Trauma alters our brain chemistry and development, making us more susceptible to conditions like high blood pressure, heart attack, stroke, dementia, and mental health disorders.[10] In short, every human needs mental healthcare because our mental well-being is one primary factor that determines our quality of life. Black people are not an exception to the rule. If anything, we are in desperate need as a people because so many of us were *conditioned* to neglect our mental and emotional health.

We have been through dreadful experiences as a race.

We are descendants of enslaved people.

We are the children of parents who didn't get the mental health treatment they needed.

We come from generations of trauma and suffering.

Many of us have not received much psychological education.

And most importantly, we are human.

Yes, Black people are resilient, but many simply survive instead of reaching their full potential partially because of the adverse effects of trauma. We all have psychological needs, and mental healing is necessary for our well-being. We cannot afford to ignore our mental health because doing so allows our trauma to continue to dictate outcomes in our lives. We must commit to getting to know ourselves intimately by learning to properly process our emotions, acknowledging what needs to be unlearned, and identifying our authentic selves.

To reach our goals, we all need healthy guidance on identifying what we need to change within ourselves and how to change it. Sometimes, we have blinders to the parts of ourselves that need healing, so seeking professional help is often an essential part of the process. I knew I needed healing and increased self-awareness, but I didn't specifically know what to do until I went to therapy.

Therapy is the application of psychology. Psychology is a science that teaches us how our experiences have shaped us, why we do what we do, and how to use that knowledge to improve our lives. Before diving into this book's primary content, I want to ensure every reader understands what psychology is and its importance regarding our mental health. Especially because, as a Black woman, I have personally heard some of the myths about mental health that afflict our communities. The rest of this chapter will summarize psychology and its imperative role in helping us understand and heal ourselves.

What Is Psychology?

Psychology, as a formal area of scientific study, began around 1854. However, the informal research of human nature existed much earlier, dating all the way back to 600 BCE.[11] Because of this rich history, we now know so much about ourselves and how to improve our mental and behavioral health. We are also continuously studying humans to learn even more! Shockingly, this information isn't taught in schools at early grade levels, despite how beneficial it can be in helping us understand and care for our mental well-being. (But I'll save my frustrations about this for another time).

Psychology is a social science partially based on other sciences that most of us respect and wholeheartedly believe in. Specifically, psychology includes elements of research from the following sciences:

- Biology and Chemistry
- Medicine, including pharmacology and health studies
- Mathematics, statistics, logic, and computer science (used for psychological research and experimentation)

- Neuroscience
- Other social sciences, including anthropology, cognitive science, political science, linguistics, sociology, and communications

Psychology is not just the work of random people espousing theories based on their opinions. Like most areas of science, it's founded on over two thousand years of human experimentation, research, observation, and tested theories. The relationship between psychology and other sciences is bidirectional. The findings from psychology influence other sciences and vice versa, which helps us better understand ourselves as humans. This relationship between the sciences is also why many significant contributors to psychology have been experts in other areas of study, including medicine, biology, genetics, philosophy, and others.

The field of psychology has studied (and explains) many types of human behavior, including, but not limited to, the following:

- Why, in group settings, we change our behavior (Asch conformity experiments) and our thoughts (groupthink)
- Why we're less likely to intervene in an emergency when other people are around (the bystander effect)
- Why we mimic the facial expressions and mannerisms of people we frequently interact with (the chameleon effect)
- Why we assume the worst of other people (fundamental attribution error)
- How powerful our thoughts and beliefs are (placebo effect, confirmation bias, etc.)
- Why marketing and manipulation strategies work on us (foot-in-the-door technique, door-in-the-face technique, etc.)
- How social media influences our emotions, behaviors, and beliefs

The list is endless, but it's simple. If it relates to human phenomena, researchers in the field of psychology have studied it. Plus, as new aspects of humanity develop, just as we did when social media became a thing, we will conduct research to learn about those topics too. The field is forever growing and adapting because humans are forever evolving.

Although I wrote *Bold. Black. & Becoming* in honor of Black mental health, psychology applies to us all. Just like medical knowledge benefits our physical well-being, psychology benefits us psychologically, behaviorally, and emotionally. Understanding it tremendously increases our self-awareness. This is imperative because we can make necessary changes when we genuinely comprehend what we do and why. It's like the ultimate cheat code for life if we are willing to learn and apply it. Not having this information is like living on autopilot, trapped in the same cycle with little understanding of why or how to change it.

I use this knowledge daily and have helped clients from all backgrounds do the same to improve their mental and behavioral health. In this book, I have highlighted some of the essential parts of psychology that I believe Black communities can benefit from the most. I hope by sharing my knowledge, others will be able to make the changes within themselves and in their lives that they desire to achieve.

CHAPTER 2

Healing Your Relationship with Yourself

*For so long, we have denied what makes us most human;
reconnecting with this part of ourselves is how we begin to heal.*

Black people have been socialized (conditioned and taught) to suppress and ignore their emotions for ages.[12] From childhood, caregivers led many of us to believe our feelings were unimportant and made us weak. I am sure this conditioning came with good intentions and was a way of trying to cope with trauma. After all, historically, we have gone through horrendous events. However, suppressing and ignoring isn't the way to go.

You may not realize it, but suppressing emotions has caused many of us to be very disconnected from ourselves and others. This suppression is also the source of several recurring problems in our lives, like unhealthy relationship patterns and poor decision-making. Suppression causes us to become less of ourselves, and we begin living life on autopilot. Our emotions are what makes us most human. Not only do we need emotions, but when we ignore them, we face terrible consequences over time.

I don't intend to give you an in-depth neuroscience lesson since that's not the purpose of this book. However, I want to explain how essential it is to have an intimate relationship with your feelings. Our brain's anatomy naturally makes us *all* emotional creatures. In other words, we are mentally hardwired to experience emotions every moment of every day. Many of us mistakenly believe having emotions is a choice. It's not; if you have a brain, you are constantly feeling something. How much you *acknowledge, express, or respond* to your emotions is up to you, but having them is not.

It's important to note that changes in our mood or emotional state are an entirely normal part of the human experience. Many parts of the human brain play a role in creating, regulating, processing, expressing, or interpreting emotion, including, but not limited to, the following parts:[13]

- Frontal lobe
- Amygdala
- Cingulate gyrus
- Hypothalamus
- Hippocampus
- Cerebral cortex

The human brain is like a snowflake: we all have the same structures and parts, but due to minor differences from person to person, no two brains are entirely identical.[14] Our emotional experiences are complex because they involve multiple brain structures. One could argue that our feelings are at the center of everything we are due to our brain anatomy. They influence our thoughts and behaviors and play a significant role in our brain's functioning. You might be thinking, "If we're all so emotional, why don't we act like it?" The answer to this question is simple: conditioning. See, internally, we all do "act like it." We all constantly experience emotions. However, differences in emotional expression depend on a person's level of self-awareness and how comfortable they are with expressing their feelings. Both are usually determined primarily by how that person was socialized or raised, which includes cultural influences. Of course, there are other factors, but in most cases, conditioning creates and sometimes sustains differences in emotional expression.

If you've been around young children, you know we all enter the world authentically and unapologetically showing emotion. Even our first sign of life depended on us expressing intense emotion, crying upon exiting the womb. We start life this way because our brains are hardwired for emotional expression, and before we're told otherwise, we show our feelings freely. For example, my two-year-old son expresses every emotional experience without hesitation and cries multiple times a day. As parents, we frequently talk to him about his emotions, and we do not shame him for having feelings because they are natural. Discipline is vital, but it shouldn't promote emotional suppression. Instead, we explore his feelings with him so he can understand them, nurturing his emotional intelligence, and we teach him healthier ways to express his feelings, nurturing his emotional regulation skills. We do this so he can one day be a highly emotionally intelligent adult, capable of creating healthy, emotionally intimate relationships with others and of having a healthy relationship with himself. We want him to feel comfortable with his feelings and have a deep understanding of how to work well with them. After all, his emotions make up an essential part of his humanity.

If you are a millennial or older, your parents probably didn't fully understand the importance of emotional intelligence. The topic was not widely discussed while they were growing up or when they were raising us. During that time, emotional suppression was the norm, and many people thought the best way to manage your emotions was to pretend like you didn't have any.

Many clients have told me they grew up rarely receiving physical affection from their parents or hearing "I love you." Instead, they constantly received unfair criticism and verbal or physical abuse. Further, even for some of my clients who did receive loving affection, their parents often provided it in an uncomfortable or limited manner, such as *only* using humor to express affection because their parents found it awkward to do so in a heartfelt way.

If you take a moment to objectively analyze how your grandparents and parents responded to and expressed their feelings, you may realize how much they struggled. In many cases, emotional suppression and neglect negatively impacted outcomes in their lives, including the quality of their relationships (especially marriages), difficulty with intimacy and showing affection, people-pleasing behaviors, anger issues, or substance abuse. It is clear that suppressing emotion damages us psychologically, contributes to adverse outcomes in our lives, and causes a significant disconnect from others and, due to decreased self-awareness, from ourselves. But when we think about it, is it really that surprising that denying and neglecting a major part of who we are causes us harm over time?

We've gotten here because of generational factors and a history of neglecting mental health. When we ignore something, we fail to understand it, and what we don't understand, we fail to appropriately respond to. In other words, parents cannot teach or instill in us what they don't *yet* know how to do for themselves. Just like a parent can't teach their child French unless they know French, a parent with severely limited emotional intelligence cannot equip their child with the knowledge and skills needed to manage their emotions. Since many of our parents attempted to use suppression to "manage" their feelings, they never actually learned effective skills to cope with and express those emotions properly.

As a millennial, I didn't *relearn* how to connect with my emotions until adulthood. (I say "relearn" because we all start life connected to our feelings.) My parents did the best they could with what they knew, but they weren't very familiar with emotional intelligence. It wasn't something their parents (or anybody else) taught them, so their relationship with their emotions was limited. As a result, they could only give me so much in this department. Going to therapy and my career as a psychologist have both helped me *build* a strong, healthy relationship with my feelings. My husband also went to individual therapy to do the same. Now, we share our growing emotional intelligence with our son so he can have a healthy relationship with his feelings too.

Growing up, we all relied on our caregivers to help us understand ourselves and our experiences. Differences in expressing and understanding our feelings began with how we were conditioned during childhood. Just as my son's does, our conditioning depended on what our caregivers told us about our feelings and how they reacted to them. It also depended on how they respond to their own emotions and their willingness to be vulnerable. Unfortunately, many of us received a lot of negative messages about our emotions during childhood (with boys often receiving some of the worst messages).

Receiving responses like the following:

- "Stop crying before I give you something to cry about!"
- "You're always so dramatic."
- "Stop acting like a little girl. Man up!"
- "Shut up and be quiet! Ain't nothing botherin' you."

Many also experienced behaviors like the following:

- Being mocked and called "too emotional or sensitive."
- Eye rolls and sighs as if our emotions were a burden or inconvenience to others.
- Discouragement from expressing intense emotion or crying, which led to the belief that expressing deep emotion was wrong or inappropriate.

- Lack of a safe space to describe how something made them feel.
- Never experienced their parent give a sincere, heartfelt apology or take accountability for their actions.
- Not being taught alternative ways to express and release their feelings or given frequent opportunities to practice emotional regulation skills.
- An expectation that they be seen but not heard.

Of course, parents are human too and allowed to have moments of dysregulation as well; no one is expecting perfection, and mistakes are inevitable. However, when these poor responses are not acknowledged, apologized for, and corrected, or worse, become the norm, this damages a child's relationship with themselves over time. The problem is that *frequent* responses like this promote toxic conditioning, which doesn't make us any less emotional but instead encourages disconnection from ourselves.

We begin denying one of the most sacred parts of our humanity.

We start feeling uncomfortable with having emotions, something we were biologically designed to have and will always experience.

We start seeing our feelings as inconvenient because others treat them that way.

We begin to struggle with our daily emotional experiences because no one ever taught us how to properly work through what we feel.

We begin to suppress, and as a result, we become less of ourselves.

Emotional Regulation

Emotional regulation is a person's ability to effectively manage and respond to the emotions they experience throughout the day. Regulating is about allowing yourself to feel, processing your feelings, and moving through them, so it is the exact *opposite* of suppressing. Just like any skill, it has to be intentionally taught over time by someone who already embodies the skill; this is how a person eventually learns how to do it on their own. Keep in mind that being skilled at something isn't the same as being perfect at it because perfection is a myth. In order to learn, we just need a teacher who is knowledgeable about, skilled at, and dedicated to doing the skill. Teaching can come in many forms, including in-person (through modeling and explanation), books, videos, etc. Plus, being taught through different methods helps us develop an ability further. Even once we become skilled, the learning never ends because all skills need to be maintained and can be continuously honed through ongoing practice.

It is important to note that learning emotional regulation doesn't mean we are meant to regulate in isolation. One of the reasons humans are biologically designed to be emotional is so that we can hold the weight of our big emotions together; this is why empathy is such an important skill to learn and nurture because it is how we connect and help each other move through heavy emotions.

Of course, not every emotional experience will require support from others. Through practice, your threshold for what you can handle on your own will increase. This is why most adults are able to regulate their emotions when they realize they are out of their favorite cereal, but a toddler would likely become emotionally dysregulated. Since they are so young and their brains are still developing, they haven't had enough time to advance to the point where they can consistently handle that kind of disappointment in a regulated way.

However, this doesn't mean that getting older guarantees that a person will be skilled at regulation. We all have three ages: biological, mental, and emotional. A person can be biologically sixty years old but mentally and emotionally still be five. Due to time and physical maturation, our biological age automatically progresses without us having to do anything. On the other hand, what we were taught during our upbringing and how dedicated we are to self-work as an adult determines whether or not we continue to grow mentally and emotionally over our lifetime.

Many adults were never taught this ability and are still unwilling to take the time to learn and nurture it. As a result, they engage in unhealthy behaviors when things don't go their way. They gaslight and project onto others. They refuse to self-reflect and take accountability. They may even get violent or verbally abusive. They react similarly to a young child because they haven't yet advanced past the basic skillset they started life with. Regardless of age, if we want to get better at something, we have to be willing to learn, practice, and allow ourselves to be taught. We also have to embrace learning as an ongoing part of life. Unfortunately, some choose to live their life believing that hitting a certain age means you no longer have anything to learn. As a result, they are resistant to feedback that could help with their self-development.

Additionally, no matter how skilled you get, some emotional experiences will almost always require support from others, such as grief, intense anger, intense sadness, etc. This is because certain events, like major traumas, take significant time to work through and often require ongoing maintenance throughout our lives. We should seek emotional support regularly from people who are skilled at giving it because we all need it. Even as adults, we still need others to help us co-regulate when we are going through something that has had a profound emotional impact on us. We must be honest with ourselves about the things that affect us, no matter what they are, because this is the only way to meet our needs and take care of our mental health.

The best way to explain how to nurture and teach the skill of emotional regulation is through a real-life example. When we enter the world, we have a limited ability to do this well. This is why my son (and all toddlers) respond to minor inconveniences as if they are a crisis. Of course, he has moments when he does manage his emotions reasonably well based on what we have taught him thus far, but overall, at two years old, he still has a very long way to go before he masters emotional regulation.

As parents, it is our job to teach and nurture this skill so he can significantly improve this ability as he grows. To do that, we must empathize with how he sees the situation and talk to him about his emotions from his perspective. By meeting him where he is, we can help him expand upon his understanding of the situation and sharpen his ability to process his experiences thoroughly and accurately. After all, when teaching someone something, we must start at their current level of understanding if we want to help them advance past it; no different than if I wanted to teach my child algebra, I would first need to make sure he could identify numbers and their values. Learning basic math alone would take significant time, repetition, and patience, which means I should expect that mastering these subjects will take even longer, especially for a human whose brain is still developing.

Even though, as adults, we know getting the purple spoon instead of the red one is not a crisis, we have to respond to him with the understanding that, in his eyes, it is. After all, when we were toddlers, we would have reacted the same way; the only reason we no longer do is because we have been alive longer and have a deeper understanding of the world. Our son just learned what a spoon was a few months ago, and this discovery is important to him, so his perspective is very different. Through explanation, patience, redirection, and empathy, he will, over time, begin to have significantly less intense feelings regarding the color of his spoon. However, for now, we have to meet him where he is, mentally and emotionally, in order to help him grow from that place.

Teaching suppression prevents a child from learning and nurturing the skill of emotional regulation. In fact, it strips them of it. If we yelled at our son and said, "It's no big deal! It's just a spoon!" we would not only increase his frustration (because yelling when someone is upset escalates emotions) but also invalidate his feelings. Yes, of course, we want him to *eventually* understand the color of the spoon is not a crisis. Still, we must first be willing to meet him where he is to get him to that realization without negatively impacting his relationship with his emotions. His feelings matter even if they differ from ours and even if we know that he will eventually see the situation differently.

Suppression would teach our son to pretend he doesn't have emotions when he clearly does. It may seem like an easy way out. Still, the consequence of teaching him to suppress would be that later in life, when emotionally triggered by something more significant, he would have limited emotional regulation skills because he didn't get what he needed during childhood. Struggling with emotional regulation as he ages would increase his risk of aggression, outbursts, anxiety, and depression. This is why helping him successfully work through the problems he faces as a toddler is vital; these experiences set the foundation for how he will manage difficult emotions caused by more complex problems in the future. Our son's toddler problems are our opportunity to teach him emotional regulation with an issue that's a cakewalk for us. Teaching suppression would be a failure to take advantage of such a vital learning opportunity for him.

Empathy is taking the time to understand someone else's perspective and feelings, an important skill we want him to have as an adult. We model empathy by helping him understand that having a color preference is totally reasonable. Even as adults, most of us have a favorite color. He is allowed to have a favorite spoon color, just like I have a favorite coffee mug. The only difference is that I've learned that the very mild disappointment I experience when I can't use that mug is simply an inconvenience; I wasn't born understanding this. My life experiences helped me better understand what my emotions are communicating to me, which allows me to have a different perspective and emotional response. He hasn't been here long enough to have achieved the same yet. Plus, it's our responsibility to teach him this.

Our son's real goal is to eat, and the color of the spoon does not prevent him from achieving this goal, just like the mug I use doesn't prevent my goal of drinking coffee. He didn't initially recognize this because the situation triggered him. His brain stopped processing when he saw the purple spoon because he associates his favorite red spoon with eating. Our job as parents is to help him go beyond that initial reaction to understand the situation better.

By modeling empathy, we not only help him regulate his emotions (because he usually calms down quickly in response to us showing compassion), but we also help him improve his problem-solving skills. Once he has calmed down a bit (because we can't learn when dysregulated), we show him he can use the purple spoon to eat. This helps him move from a crisis mindset to an inconvenience mindset, which helps him regulate. We also let him know he can use his red spoon for dinner, which continues to model empathy and validates his emotions and preferences. When we help him through his emotional experiences and provide a safe space to feel, he learns how to empathize, solve problems, and respond (instead of react) to his feelings over time.

Of course, we have to *consistently* respond to his needs this way for him to improve these skills; doing so once is not sufficient. The more we respond this way, the better he gets at it. (And guess what! He has fewer outbursts, making our job easier over time!) As humans, we all benefit from repetition and consistency when it comes to learning something new. We rarely master something from being taught once, regardless of age. Sooner than later, our son will respond to not having his favorite spoon like I do to not having my favorite coffee mug. If we taught him to suppress, he would feel foolish about preferring the red spoon and continue to struggle with emotional regulation when bigger problems arise. In other words, it would negatively impact his self-esteem and deprive him of an important life skill.

Although minor, this spoon preference is part of his individuality and self-discovery as a toddler. He'll likely grow up and not care what color his spoon is, but we don't want it to be because we made him feel like his feelings didn't matter. *If he grows up not to care, we want it to be because of his self-discovery and increased understanding of the world.* If the color red makes him happy, that's part of who he is, and as his parents, it's exciting to see more of his individuality. We want to preserve his self-expression while also helping him regulate his emotions and learn the difference between a crisis and an inconvenience. We want him to be self-aware and self-assured. Nurturing these traits gets him closer to being an emotionally in-tune and well-adjusted adult skilled at emotional regulation and confident in owning who he is.

> It has been months since I wrote this section of the book, and ultimately, it only took *three breakfasts* with a different colored spoon (and our consistent response to him) before our son was able to understand that the color of the spoon was just a minor inconvenience. He no longer cares which spoon he uses, but he still loves the color red as of now. However, yellow is becoming a quick favorite due to his newfound love for ducks!)

Emotional Intelligence

Emotional intelligence represents your ability to understand, use, and manage emotions beneficially. It results from having your emotional needs met during your upbringing (or later in life if your parents did not fully provide what you needed). Lower emotional intelligence makes navigating life, especially relationships and emotional experiences, significantly difficult. A person with high emotional intelligence is skilled at relieving stress, empathizing with others, communicating effectively, resolving conflict, being vulnerable, and successfully working through life's challenges.

So many adults struggle to manage and cope with their feelings because they didn't receive what they needed in childhood and adolescence. When emotional regulation and emotional intelligence are fostered from birth, people continuously grow in these abilities over the years. After all, consistently practicing skills is how we get better at them. This way, by the time we reach adulthood, we are well-equipped to manage the emotions that come from adult problems. Failing to nurture these abilities early on causes adults to be left with toddler-like, "spoon crisis" coping skills while faced with adult issues. Clearly, that's a major problem! We see it playing out in society every day. Adult temper tantrums look like screaming and cursing, gun violence, physical assaults, punching walls, and road rage.

Adult temper tantrums are not the only consequence of lower emotional intelligence. People who struggle to manage their emotions also turn to unhealthy coping behaviors, such as substance abuse, compulsive spending, self-harm, overeating, unprotected and impulsive sex, and other avoidance behaviors.[15] This has gone on for so many generations that until recently, many people believed teaching emotional suppression was the goal (and unfortunately, many still do). In reality, teaching and encouraging emotional suppression is a type of trauma with lasting negative psychological, emotional, behavioral, and physical consequences. Suppression is one of the worst traumas because it profoundly impacts every aspect of a person's life. Without realizing it, generations of people have socialized children to grow into emotionally incompetent adults who struggle to comprehend and manage their feelings, ultimately putting them at an increased risk of developing severe mental and behavioral health disorders.

The undeniable truth is that we cannot fully understand ourselves by ignoring parts of the human experience, especially something as constant as our emotions. We cannot learn to work with our feelings if we deny their importance and disregard them. That would be like expecting someone to become a master mechanic without ever allowing them to look under the hood of a car. We were never meant to suppress what we feel, and, as a people, we have suffered gravely for it.

From birth, the true goal was to evolve how we expressed our emotions and to increase our understanding of them (i.e., emotional regulation and emotional intelligence)—learning to work with them, not against them, because they are a part of us whether we like it or not. Our feelings are energy, so we face undesirable consequences when we hold them inside (especially negative emotions). Acknowledging our emotions allows us to work through and with them, eventually releasing them. When we hold them in, they amplify and slowly affect our health. Consequently, we also fail to learn essential skills that help us manage them well because we have to practice working with our feelings in order to actually learn. Being deeply in touch with our emotions allows us to connect deeply with ourselves and others, which enables us to navigate life better.

Seven Truths about Emotions

Of course, because of differences in our conditioning, every person reading *Bold. Black. & Becoming* is in a different place in their relationship with their feelings. I want to share seven truths we must accept if we're going to improve our relationship with ourselves, regardless of where we are on our healing journey.

Truth #1. We are emotional creatures. It's not optional. How we choose to express our emotions is a choice, but having feelings is not. The only way to achieve being "emotionless" would be to literally take our brains out of our heads, but obviously, we need them for survival, so that's not an option.

Truth #2. Our emotions, even the crappy ones, are our friends. Self-awareness and our emotions go hand in hand. Deeply understanding our feelings is how we achieve heightened self-awareness. People who frequently suppress their emotions live life on autopilot;

they don't know what they're feeling or why they do what they do. If you ask them, they'll likely say they understand their feelings, but because they're so emotionally disconnected, they've lost touch with themselves. They may have a surface-level understanding but struggle to comprehend the complex nature of their emotions. Living like this can lead to a person repeatedly finding themselves in the same undesirable situations while struggling to figure out what to do differently. This is one of the negative consequences of emotional disconnect.

Without emotional awareness, we are guaranteed to have more life challenges. Our emotions exist for a reason: they communicate important things to us! They help guide us and are essential for good decision-making when appropriately used (more on this in the next chapter). But this can only happen when we understand our emotions and take the time to get comfortable with them. Otherwise, neglecting them leads to our feelings working against us.

Truth #3. Our emotions do not make us weak. They make us human. We all have them, so either we are all weak *or* experiencing emotions is just part of who we are. Science and the composition of the human brain strongly support the "it's who we are" explanation, so this is undebatable. Suppressing our emotions may seem like the easier route, but it has dire consequences that aren't worth it in the long run.

Learning to be comfortable with feeling and healthily expressing our emotions is one of the strongest things we can do. There's nothing weak about it. Feeling our feelings is often really hard. That's why so many people try to avoid it. If feeling our emotions were easy, nobody would be tempted to suppress them in the first place. It takes significant strength and vulnerability to feel. I have never been more challenged than when I am faced with the task of feeling heavy emotions.

Suppression is a cop-out. When we allow ourselves to get acquainted with our feelings and use them how they were intended to be used, that's strength! Learning to do so improved my life tremendously, and it will do the same for you. Nothing good comes from denying who we are or what we feel. When we suppress, we are working against our biology; that's why there are so many negative consequences. We don't give ourselves or our bodies what we need when we refuse to feel our emotions.

Truth #4. Suppression is psychologically and physically toxic.
When we chronically suppress our feelings, they become a mental toxin to us. This is not an opinion. It's a scientific fact with endless data to support it. It's never good when we allow anything to build up, and our emotions are no different. Our emotions are meant to be released, not held on to. When we swallow them, they affect us negatively over time.

Think about it. If emotions were unnecessary, all the centuries of emotional suppression would have led to advancements for humans, but instead, the opposite has occurred. Emotional suppression, limited emotional intelligence, and limited self-awareness are scientifically linked to the following:

- Addictive behaviors, including substance abuse
- Relational violence and anger issues
- Suicide
- Mood disorders
- Chronic feelings of loneliness due to being emotionally disconnected from others and not having emotionally intimate relationships
- Health problems like stroke, high blood pressure, heart disease, gastrointestinal issues, and even Alzheimer's disease
- Racism, homophobia, and other forms of hate (due to a lack of empathy for others, which is a major part of emotional intelligence)
- Chronic stress and the development of stress-related disorders
- Changes to brain chemistry, especially the nervous and cardiovascular systems

Unfortunately, there are plenty of other associated negative outcomes. In short, chronically suppressing emotions hurts us mentally and physically and makes the world worse.

Long ago, we discovered the correlation between poor mental and physical health. I often think about how the statistics for various psychological and physical health disorders would drastically decrease if people were taught how to take better care of their emotional health. Years of emotional suppression takes a drastic toll on the body and the brain. In theory, so many people could have avoided developing certain conditions if they'd only had the opportunity to establish a healthy relationship with themselves. It's genuinely heartbreaking.

Truth #5. Suppressing our emotions is a choice, but so is feeling them. Our emotional experiences are automatic. They show up without our permission, but once we become consciously aware of them, we get to decide what we do. We can respond in many ways, but the one thing I hope you will rarely choose is to suppress. Throughout this book, we will discuss different emotions and what they are calling us to do. Allow yourself to listen to their messages because they exist for a reason, and what they tell you is important.

Truth #6. Crying is healthy and imperative for our well-being. Crying was the first thing you did when you entered the world, and you were never meant to cease doing it altogether. We are biologically designed to cry as a way to release big emotions, which helps us regulate; this is why so many adults are frequently dysregulated, as they refuse to process and release. Of course, being taught the skill of emotional regulation (not suppression) changes how often we need to cry because we begin to be affected by things differently (just like my son stopped caring about the color of his spoons). However, becoming more skilled at regulating includes understanding the vital role crying plays when something actually has a profound impact on us for whatever reason. Suppression doesn't allow for the release that we desperately need. Instead, it makes us numb and dysregulated, which often leads to irrational thoughts and behaviors.

Crying is *not* about sadness; it is about emotional awareness and intense emotional release. Any emotion can make us cry if it is strong enough, dependent on the circumstances: we would cry if we won the lottery, if someone we love did something thoughtful for us, if we see an emotional scene in a movie, or if we are feeling overwhelmed. There is no "wrong" reason, and our need to cry will vary depending on a multitude of factors. We can and should cry in response to *any* emotion that evokes that need based on its intensity at the time. It is not our choice to make; when our brain and body tell us that this is what we need, we must honor it.

As part of your healing, you must remind yourself of how you started life. If you are currently uncomfortable with crying, that is a trauma response. Who taught you to invalidate your feelings? Who taught you that it wasn't okay to release or express them? Someone in your life responded poorly to your emotions. As a result, you now feel discomfort with something you were designed to do for a purpose. A major part of healing comes from observing young children so we can identify what needs to be fixed within us. When we recognize how our trauma has impacted us, we can recondition and unlearn the toxic mindsets and behaviors that the trauma caused. We must reparent ourselves so we can reclaim parts of us that we were never meant to abandon in the first place. The only way to stop the cycle of generational trauma is to choose to heal and reunite with what is healthy.

From this day forward, begin breaking the conditioning of apologizing for your feelings. Stop yourself from saying, "I'm sorry," and just allow yourself to cry when you need to. It will take time to get used to it again, but with practice and by improving your self-talk, you will get back to seeing crying as normal and natural, the way you saw it as a child before the toxic conditioning. Someone overreacting to you crying is simply a reflection of their trauma and how much healing they still need to do. Remind them that crying is not only okay but very important. Taking care of your mental health is not something to apologize for, and we need to stop making people feel weird about releasing what needs to be released. *That's what we are supposed to do!* People need to be met with empathy and safety when they are being vulnerable, not judgment. *We have to model what needs to change by being the change.* Retrain yourself to cry and allow others to cry with you.

When we say "don't cry," we are telling a person to suppress and bottle up what they feel. It may not be our intention, but it is us invalidating their feelings and declaring that we are unwilling to provide a safe space for them to feel with us. If someone else crying makes you cry, that's okay! That means you are connecting and empathizing. It means you are creating a safe space and holding the weight of the emotion with them, which helps them feel supported and less alone. It also means that you are allowing yourself to release, which is excellent for your mental health. Feeling together makes our relationships stronger! We are designed to feel and cry together; doing so is how we form deeper connections with each other. This is also why it is so unfulfilling to be in a relationship with someone emotionally unavailable and disconnected from themselves. When embraced, regulated, and properly learned about, emotions help us thrive!

Crying should be seen the way you see coughing when you need to cough or eating when hungry. It is a *biological need* that helps us care for our mental health, and when we deny it, we put ourselves at risk over time. When we cry, it means that we are allowing ourselves to feel what needs to be deeply felt; it releases those emotions in a healthy way instead of suppressing them within us. Nothing that our bodies naturally do is shameful, especially something that is meant to help us care for ourselves. Feelings are natural, and crying is too. As I said, you have been crying since day one, and this ability was meant to help you meet your emotional needs throughout your life, so it is crucial to get back in touch.

Truth #7. We have to feel more if we want to feel better. That may be surprising, but it makes sense. If suppression is linked to negative consequences, processing our emotions must lead to positive outcomes. When we process our feelings, we can work through them. What we don't acknowledge or talk about ends up affecting us subconsciously. The key is to learn how to process them intentionally and effectively; after all, doing so is a skill, and I hope that this book will help you improve this ability.

What Happens in Your Mind When You Suppress

Imagine your mind is a room you're in charge of. Since your emotions show up without your permission, they enter the room (your mind) as they please. You can't lock the door; even if you could, they would come through the window. The only thing in your control is what you do after they show up. Once they get in, you must decide whether you will acknowledge their presence and engage with them. They will still be in the room with you even if you choose to do neither.

Imagine something happens to you that causes hurt and disappointment to enter the room. You decide to ignore them because you wish they weren't there. So you turn your back on them and entertain the emotions you like, such as happiness. Hurt and disappointment quickly recognize they are being ignored, and it pisses them off. After all, they matter just as much as your positive emotions.

Hurt and disappointment are now in the part of the room you have your back turned to. This blind spot represents your subconscious. Seeking "revenge," these ignored emotions begin affecting you subconsciously by influencing your behaviors, your thoughts, and other emotions without your full awareness. Some part of you knows they're in the room, but you still refuse to turn around and acknowledge them. Because of this, they get to control you instead of you being in charge of them.

Over time, you become angry and irritable because of the influence hurt and disappointment have over you. (Anger is often a mask we use to avoid feeling more vulnerable emotions like hurt and disappointment.) You start to convince yourself this is just your attitude instead of acknowledging the deeper cause. Sure, you accept that anger has entered the room (which is good!), but you still don't address hurt or disappointment (which is bad). Anger feels safer, but refusing to acknowledge what caused the anger in the first place prevents you from working through all that you feel.

Of course, the actual cause of your mood and behavior shifts is the hurt and disappointment you never dealt with. They're running wild and free through your subconscious mind, and they're still furious that you've ignored them. They want to know why they aren't important to you. Why don't you treat them the way you treat happiness? After all, they're a part of you too.

They begin to feel unstoppable, and you desperately try to find an easy out for some sense of relief. The more time goes on, the more hurt and disappointment demand your attention by acting out further. They flip tables, throw things, and scream. They will continue to make your life hell until you acknowledge them. You start drinking more and use sex as a distraction--*anything* to get some relief. You just want them to leave already! However, these avoidance behaviors only provide temporary respite and cause more emotions to enter, leading to even more chaos in your mind because there are no shortcuts to healing. The only way to regain control is to acknowledge all the emotions in your room, to connect and engage with them.

When you suppress, you significantly decrease self-awareness. You also create more work for yourself in the long run. Talking to the hurt and disappointment would help you understand what brought them there in the first place. Suppression leads to more undesired emotions, and you have to deal with the damage hurt and disappointment caused while you were ignoring them. If you want to avoid this, you must take accountability for your whole room and everything in it, not just the parts you like.

Now, imagine you were honest with yourself when hurt and disappointment first arrived. This would have allowed you to identify your needs, process your emotions, and continue to manage your room appropriately. Like most negative emotions, hurt and disappointment do not go away quickly. They will be there for a while as you work through them. It takes time, but by choosing to monitor your room, you can keep an eye on them. You can notice how they affect you and intervene if needed. You can communicate their existence to others, tell people how you feel, and self-advocate to meet your needs. You can seek help and support if those feelings become too challenging to manage on your own. You never lose control or lose sight of them because you've chosen to manage your whole room, not just part of it, and this keeps you self-aware. And guess what? Because they were tended to appropriately, they eventually leave on their own.

Ignoring what's in our room only prolongs our recovery and healing. This is why therapy is effective and beneficial for so many people. Around seventy-five percent of people who start therapy experience some benefit from it.[16] Treatment requires people to safely address everything in their room (the mind) and learn about the emotional impact of their experiences. When we are ready to do the work, therapy with the *right* therapist can help us regain control of our room and learn the skills to manage it better going forward. As a psychologist, I've helped people regain control and unpack their rooms too many times to count. I also unpack my own room with my therapist. It's wonderful getting rid of the mental clutter holding me back from healing and growing.

Accepting the seven truths about our emotions can help us improve and heal our relationship with ourselves. We get to know ourselves better when we embrace, process, understand, and express our emotions. The better we know ourselves, the better we can navigate life. If you've found yourself frequently suppressing, thankfully, this is a learned behavior you can unlearn. You began life in touch with your emotions, so you just need to regain connection. After all, your emotions are still part of you, even if you've ignored them. They have always been in the room. It will just take practicing skills to help you get reacquainted.

How to Feel Your Emotions

Start by challenging yourself to feel more. You'll have plenty of opportunities to practice every day. When you want to change something about yourself, first, you must commit to holding yourself accountable. How you think impacts your behavior, so when you continue to self-define the same way, you give yourself no opportunity to change. In short, if you keep telling yourself you'll always be a certain way, that belief becomes a self-fulfilling prophecy (more on this in chapter 7). The first step toward change is to tell yourself you're willing to do things differently by accepting that 1) how you respond to your emotions is a choice and 2) you are now ready to choose differently.

Whenever you want to learn something new, you must practice. Speak to yourself, aloud or in your head, to remind yourself that you are working toward responding differently to feeling emotion. Hold yourself accountable for doing so every day. You won't be perfect at it, nor do you need to be. But with practice, you will inevitably get better.

Follow these two steps to improve self-awareness and emotion identification. First, feel your emotions by noticing sensations within your body. When your mood shifts or you experience intense emotion, bring your attention to your physical self. What do you notice? Has your heart rate changed? Are you feeling hot or sweaty? Are you feeling tense? Do you have butterflies in your stomach? Observing changes in your physical sensations can help you better understand what emotions you may be experiencing.

Next, allow yourself to become more aware of your thoughts. Your thoughts are the gatekeepers to your emotions and behaviors. How you speak to yourself about your experiences directly impacts your feelings. Everything starts with your thoughts, which lead to certain emotions that then influence your behaviors. For instance, if someone you waved at doesn't wave back and you think to yourself, "They did that on purpose," you are more likely to experience negative emotions like anger. However, if you think, "Oh, they must not have seen me," you are more likely to experience positive or neutral emotions. To better understand and feel your feelings more deeply, you must analyze the thoughts that led to them. By being more aware of your internal narrative and changing your thought patterns when needed, you can improve your ability to regulate your emotions.

Also, please remember that sometimes, an emotional shift is primarily caused by a hormonal shift. This is something all humans experience from time to time, and it happens for various reasons. When this occurs, acknowledge that the source of these emotions is coming from momentary changes in your brain chemistry. This can help you normalize the experience and not feed into it in a way that increases distress. For instance, if every time you feel sad, you assume it will lead to depression, you will unintentionally prime your brain for a depressive episode. We want to acknowledge what we feel and determine how to care for our needs based on those feelings. When you have a hormonal shift, recognize it as such, approach it with curiosity, and determine how you can best meet your needs so you can move through what you are feeling. Meeting your needs will almost always include engaging in various forms of self-care while you are working through the hard time. Responding this way helps decrease the likelihood of things worsening.

Accept that your old automatic responses are part of the change process. Committing to change is the first step, but expecting the old response to never happen again would be irrational. It takes time to unlearn and replace a habit; the old behavior is part of the change process. If suppression has been your go-to for years, expect to be tempted to do it when intense emotions arise. At this point, your brain has become accustomed to it despite its adverse effects. To change it, you have to replace the automatic response with the new one of feeling what you feel. Please do not beat yourself up or consider it a failure when you have your old automatic response. Instead, when it happens, see it as another opportunity to correct, unlearn, and practice. Be kind to yourself. Like riding a bike, the more you practice, the better you get! Take every opportunity as it comes.

When you find yourself shutting down, see that as a sign that the habit of suppressing is on the horizon. Whether you feel like crying but hold back your tears, or you feel upset but force a fake smile, it's a wake-up call! Even if, by the time you notice it, you have already begun engaging in suppression, you can shift gears as soon as you become consciously aware of what you're doing. Sometimes, you will catch yourself beforehand, and other times, while in the act, each is still an opportunity to work toward growth! Even if you don't realize it until after, it's still not too late. Just like I have clients who come to therapy and finally process emotions from events that happened decades ago, there is no expiration date on our feelings. The key is to commit to making time to process them as soon as possible, even if you can't do so in the moment or immediately after.

Early on, when you're working toward change, it's normal to catch yourself in or after the act instead of before it. Allow yourself to view this as part of the change process. Even if you don't realize it until afterward, there is always an opportunity to correct the behavior. Thankfully, it does not matter when we catch ourselves as long as we do! Stay committed to change by consciously reminding yourself that you're allowing your brain to break the association it has formed between feeling emotions and shutting down, which takes time. Then, allow yourself to practice exploring your feelings and expressing them healthily, using assertive, thoughtful communication (more on this in chapter 10).

When you avoid feeling your emotions, especially the positive ones, you deprive yourself of one of life's richest experiences. The best way to explain this point is by using a personal example. On my wedding day, I unapologetically cried like a baby. I allowed myself to be overwhelmed by the happiness I felt marrying the love of my life. I sensed the love and joy radiating through my body. It was euphoric! (This type of intense emotional experience can be rare. I didn't feel this amount of elation again until we were in the delivery room meeting our son two years later.)

After the ceremony, a couple of people asked me why I was still crying (I know. Crazy, right!? But this is how disconnected some people are from their emotions). Here I was, minding my business, blissfully sitting in my feelings and soaking up all they had to give. But watching me freely show emotion made some people uncomfortable because they didn't want to feel their own. They were fighting a war in their minds, and they believed shutting me down would be a quick fix.

I respectfully told them to leave me alone, which took them aback. But here's the thing. Their disconnection from themselves and their desire not to feel was not my problem to solve. By setting a boundary, I protected my peace and prevented negative emotions from coming up for me. (As we've discussed, once emotions show up, you have to deal with them if you want to be mentally healthy). I refused to let anyone stop me from experiencing all the emotional warmth from that special day. Allowing myself to be emotional wasn't a threat to anyone. I felt sorry that they failed to understand how priceless it is to have a healthy relationship with their feelings.

If I had decided to stop myself from crying or feeling "too deeply," I would have wasted so much of the day suppressing, which is emotionally draining! It's like trying to stop yourself from coughing when you desperately need to; my body was calling me to feel! Why would I want to dilute this once-in-a-lifetime experience and exhaust myself by suppressing my feelings? It takes a lot of energy to hold back emotion, and I refused to waste my energy doing something that would take away from the day.

Imagine if I could not feel anything on my wedding day. Without emotional awareness, it would have just been another day. Emotions make experiences meaningful and impactful. The love, excitement, serenity, and pure joy *made* that day. Also, sharing and experiencing those deep emotions with my husband took it to another level. We both wanted to take it all in and bask in it. Those who chose to feel with us only amplified our emotional experience, and for those who chose not to, we told them to leave us be and let us be great!

Sharing emotional energy with other humans is one of life's purest joys and necessities. When we connect emotionally like we were *intended and designed* to do, it allows us to feel connected in our humanity, and it adds so much to our experiences. This is even true for negative emotions because feeling together enables us to share the weight of those feelings and support one another as we move through them. Again, this is why empathy is such an important and invaluable skill that all humans should be taught throughout their upbringing.

We were not meant to carry the weight of our big emotions (positive or negative) alone, and this is why suppression has caused so much suffering. We have accidentally created a world of humans pretending to be robots, and we desperately need to start correcting this mistake by healing our relationship with ourselves. This will also simultaneously heal our relationships with one another because as we heal, our responses and interactions improve.

> **Brain fact:** Humans have better long-term memory for experiences that cause intense emotion, especially when we allow ourselves to feel. Our memories of our wedding day are fresh in our minds because we chose to feel deeply and unapologetically.

There is a reason we enter the world feeling and expressing ourselves, but being conditioned by others to feel uncomfortable about something so natural and biological dilutes the human experience. When we choose to suppress (especially positive emotion), we choose to make our lives duller; our feelings add color to what would otherwise be a dull existence. I don't know about you, but I want the colors of my life to be rich and vibrant!

I want to connect with those I love as deeply as I can.

To cry freely so I can feel the intense relief that crying brings.

To explore my emotions and benefit from what they add to my existence.

To know myself intimately so I can better navigate my life.

To return to how I started and what I was always meant to be: human.

So I choose to feel, and I hope you will too.

Diluting positive emotions puts you at risk. Minimizing positive emotional experiences and primarily focusing on negative ones takes a toll on the human psyche, increasing the risk of mood disorders like depression and anxiety. Embracing all your feelings as they come and healthily processing them is how you best protect your mental health.

Generally speaking, there are more opportunities to feel positive emotions, like joy and excitement, or neutral emotions, like indifference and acceptance, than there are to feel negative ones, thankfully! The problem is we often mistakenly miss out on the many opportunities to sit in positive feelings because we take them for granted or because our internal dialogue has become pessimistic. Whether experiencing the sunshine on your skin, conversing with your best friend, or reminiscing about a special memory, don't forget to take a second to notice the positive feelings the moment creates.

It's so easy to go through the motions and miss the joy daily experiences bring us. Remember to consciously think about what you are feeling and what you are grateful for. Because of your free will, you decide whether you allow yourself to notice your emotions when they happen. No matter how often you have these daily positive experiences, I hope you will choose not to take them for granted. Soak up all the happiness they bring!

You can practice feeling more deeply even with your day-to-day emotions that aren't as intense. When you step outside and feel the fresh air enter your nostrils, allow yourself to focus on the positive feelings it creates for you and how grateful you are to be able to breathe fresh air. It is so easy to take our day-to-day blessings for granted, but imagine what it would be like not to be able to take in that breath or the beautiful nature around you. You have to permit yourself to be present and choose to hold on to the happiness a moment brings. Otherwise, it's quickly fleeting. It doesn't mean you have to be mindful of every single breath you take (that would be counterproductive because that would be an overwhelming task), but it does mean it is essential to choose to be aware of it more often. When was the last time you took a moment to do something like that? Committing to doing it more frequently is how we nurture feelings of gratitude for things we would otherwise take for granted and how we feel more positive emotions. And the more we take in the positive in our lives, the more energy we will have to respond to the negative appropriately.

Follow these three steps to feel more deeply:

1. Be curious about what is causing the emotion to arise.
2. Analyze how it makes you feel.
3. If it's a positive emotion, find ways to have more moments that create the same feeling. If it's negative, determine what it's telling you about your needs and how to respond to the situation effectively.

Be prepared to have people look at you sideways for feeling your feelings. As frustrating as that can be, one thing is inevitable: when you evolve, not everyone will support or understand your growth. So many people neglect their emotions and are limited in their self-awareness. Be prepared to be judged. Be prepared to be called sensitive. Anyone mocking you for being in touch with your emotions is simply uncomfortable with theirs. Your feelings overwhelm them because they can't handle their own.

I often remind myself of this to avoid reverting to unhealthy suppression in response to negative comments and reactions. Until the world accepts what we require to be mentally and emotionally healthy, those striving to achieve this goal must navigate interactions with those who aren't yet. We must decide what is more important to us, doing what's healthiest or being concerned about what others might think about it. We don't control other people, so we can't stop them from judging. However, we do control ourselves, and through practice, we can become comfortable even when others don't understand.

Remember: our thoughts are the gatekeepers to our emotions and behaviors. It's all about changing our mindset and understanding the value of doing so. Now, this doesn't mean you won't still experience negative emotions in response to their poor responses (because you will sometimes – you're human, and emotions are automatic), but with the right mindset, it can help you process and move through those emotions well; this is the goal. We can't stop ourselves from having emotions, but through practice, we can become better at responding to and moving through them. I still have this happen from time to time as well because there is no such thing as being unbothered, and when people act this way, it's hurtful and disappointing. However, I have seen over the years that my ability to work through these feelings efficiently and effectively only improves as I continue to better my mindset regarding these interactions.

Furthermore, setting boundaries is essential to protecting yourself from misguided judgments. Often, when you analyze the lives of those criticizing you for feeling, it is clear how much they struggle because they refuse to do the same. Don't let other people stop you from having a deep relationship with yourself; your quality of life depends on it. You cannot allow people who don't wish to improve their mental health to stop you from improving yours. What matters most is nurturing your relationship with your mind and emotions by being fully engaged. The more curious about and invested in exploring your feelings and thoughts you are, the better you understand yourself and can work toward healing. That will make you healthier and improve your life. Outside of that, all you can do is wish the best for people who judge you and send good vibes that they will work toward healing one day.

If (or should I say when) you experience someone like this, set a boundary to protect yourself, like I did at my wedding. Protect your peace. Don't continue to engage if it's causing emotional distress. As you embark on this journey of self-healing, it is imperative to remember it's not safe to open up to just anyone. Seek out emotionally intelligent people so you have safe spaces to feel. Whether with your partner, best friend, or therapist, the goal is to create as many emotionally safe relationships as possible. These types of connections allow you space to process and better understand your experiences. They also allow you to get your emotional needs met by others, which is essential for mental stability.

When you have interactions that don't feel supportive, don't forget to process how the person made you feel once it's safe to do so. Again, you don't want to suppress. Your emotions are like a Sour Patch Kid: sweet to you when you pay attention to them and sour when you don't. When you work through your feelings, you can prevent them from negatively affecting your life. Remember to acknowledge your feelings, process them, and increase your self-understanding.

Talking about your feelings is not the same as complaining. Many of us have been accused of complaining when sharing our emotions. These accusations encourage the false belief that discussing these things is somehow wrong when, in reality, discussing our feelings is the only thing stopping all conversation from staying surface-level. Sadly, the people who say you're complaining are often the most emotionally suppressed. They're so overwhelmed by years of self-neglect that emotional conversations feel triggering.

In general, expressing our emotions and thoughts is not complaining. But sometimes it is, and that's not necessarily a bad thing! There are two main definitions of the word complain: 1) to express annoyance or dissatisfaction about something and 2) to state that one is suffering from pain, grief, or other symptoms of unwellness.[17]

Should we not be allowed to express our annoyance, dissatisfaction, pain, or grief? Aren't these significant human experiences that deserve to be spoken about too? When we feel these feelings, we have every right to complain. Sure, we want to be mindful not to engage in negativity bias and get stuck in a loop of constantly complaining about everything, so much so that we neglect to acknowledge the positive in our lives. But complaining, when done in an emotionally congruent manner, is not problematic. Somewhere along the way, the word "complain" began to have a negative connotation that is not part of the original definition. This word simply represents the expression of many challenging emotional states that deserve recognition.

Get back in touch with who you were before other people influenced you. Think back to who you were as a child. Who you were before the trauma. Before the world told you your individuality wasn't okay and tried to make you a replica of others. What did you like? How did you express yourself? What were your favorite things about yourself? Get back in touch with your inner child because that part of you is the foundation for your authentic self.

If you don't remember who you were before the trauma (and even if you do), challenge yourself to try new things—experiment with how you express yourself. Test things out to see what you like or don't like. Keep an open mind and remain curious. Seek out new knowledge and allow others to challenge your beliefs respectfully. Try to get back in touch with your childlike wonder.

Work on identifying your trauma responses and be sure to unlearn them to get in touch with your authentic self. Don't stop learning about who you are because it's a task that cannot be completed in one lifetime. There's always something new to learn or another way to grow! Humans are complex, so getting to know yourself is a never-ending journey if you do it right.

Consider finding the right therapist for you. Of course, going to therapy is entirely your choice. As I stated in the introduction of this book, I can't account for every reader's experience with the information I'm providing. However, therapy offers a safe space to dive into your life to understand how you've gotten to where you are and to unlearn what you need to unlearn.

Therapy can help you figure out how you became the person you are and identify areas of change to become who you want to be. It allows you to heal your trauma so it can no longer negatively impact your life. It provides a space to analyze your current relationships and identify unhealthy ones. It gives you the knowledge of psychology to better understand yourself and others, and it can give you so much more!

Therapists are not "one size fits all." The right therapist for you will be one you can genuinely connect with and feel comfortable with, at least after a couple of sessions. They will be competent in treating the concerns that brought you to therapy, and they will lovingly challenge you. They will also teach you skills to practice outside of sessions and will provide a lot of psychoeducation. If something feels off, please share this with your therapist and allow them to address your concerns, and please seek someone new if it still doesn't feel like a good fit after a few sessions. As with any healthcare professional, finding the right person for you sometimes takes trial and error.

If you want to take better care of yourself, you must reconnect with any other part of you that you hide out of fear of not being enough or not fitting in. You must be willing to express yourself even if other people don't understand. One of humanity's biggest mistakes is forcing people into boxes where they don't belong. Just like we are hardwired to be emotional creatures from birth, we are also hardwired to be our authentic selves. We have misguidedly tried to make the world black-and-white, but in reality, it is gray. None of us are meant to be exactly alike, and we have mistakenly tried to erase our individuality for the sake of conformity. Everyone deserves the world to be a safe space for them to live their truth.

Listen to yourself. Pay attention to what makes you happy and to the things and people that attract you. Your uniqueness makes you beautiful, and embracing it is the key to life satisfaction and happiness. No longer suppress the natural parts of you that make you who you are because you are the one who suffers if you do. Trust that you will find the right people by seeking and being selective. When you commit to self-betterment and living authentically, you choose to live your happiest life, which is precisely the type of life you deserve to live.

CHAPTER 3

Be Response-Focused

*It only takes a few seconds to analyze a problem, so
put the rest of your energy into responding to it.*

U nsurprisingly, when our experiences fail to nurture our growth, it increases the risk of us being severely affected in the long term. It's similar to how bullying affects children. Some bullied children will eventually receive help and do the work to heal from the negative messages they received. While others, unfortunately, will grow into adults who are still very psychologically harmed by those experiences. Even though they are just as capable as the other children who recovered from the trauma, they haven't received the tools or support they need to do the same healing work.

Having multiple negative experiences can cause a person to feel disempowered, making it harder for them to reach their full potential. This is due to the relationship between our thoughts, emotions, and behaviors. Having multiple adverse experiences shifts our mindset, causing more negative emotions and helplessness behaviors, which consequently leads to more negative experiences (which, of course, then causes more negative thoughts, feelings, and behaviors, creating a harmful psychological cycle). Over time, negative experiences can impact our locus of control, how much control we believe we have over ourselves, and the outcomes in our lives.

A person can have either an internal or external locus of control. Research has shown that because of the higher risk of negative experiences, Black people are more susceptible to having an external locus of control, believing they don't have much influence or power over the outcomes in their lives.[18] Such a belief, whether conscious or subconscious, directly impacts a person's choices, self-esteem, and chances of success.

Despite hardship, our power over our lives is astounding because we have free will. Accepting this reality gives us an internal locus of control. One way to achieve an internal locus of control is by being response-focused instead of problem-focused when life throws a dilemma our way. When we accept the power we have over ourselves, our choices, and the outcomes in our lives, we put in a deliberate effort toward our goals, even when experiencing self-doubt or fear. We continue working toward our ambitions even after experiencing failure. We do not allow one or a few failures to define us. Instead, we view failure as a learning opportunity that can help us redirect.

With an internal locus of control, we are less likely to feel hopeless when creating a life we desire for ourselves. We feel capable when confronted with a challenge or difficulty. We remain curious and open-minded to new information as it can help us increase our understanding of ourselves and the world. We value what we *need* to do over what we *want* to do, and we are willing to seek help and support from others who can help us achieve our goals.

An internal locus of control is simply a mindset, so regardless of life experiences, anyone can train themselves to think this way. To shift to or maintain an internal locus of control, you must accept that, *for the most part*, life is not just happening to you. Instead, most of what happens in your life results from your choices, which means you can improve your life by making better choices. You must also accept that a smaller portion of life does include events that *genuinely* just happen to you, but you still have some control because you decide how you respond to those events.

I am by no means trying to downplay how challenging life can be. Societal barriers create undeniable challenges that make it significantly harder to thrive. But this is also why it is even more imperative that our mindset is not an additional barrier. We need our state of mind to be empowering and a reflection of just how capable we are if we are going to face the challenges that life can bring. If both the outside world and our mentality are barriers, then this significantly harms our chances of changing our circumstances. Working on developing an internal locus of control helps you identify all that's in your power and the gradual steps you can take to make your goals a reality. The world is not fully in your control, but your mindset and choices are, so practicing this skill is the best use of your energy.

When confronted with a problem or hardship (losing a job, a relationship ending, etc.), you should first acknowledge and analyze the impact of it. Of course, we usually do this automatically; however, many people stop here, causing them to be problem-focused. In other words, they obsess over the problem, and the longer they do this, the less in control they feel. After all, continuously focusing only on the problem tends to make us feel defeated and hopeless over time.

Instead of focusing all your energy on the dilemma, shift your energy to your ability to respond to it. Again, *thoroughly* analyzing the problem is an essential first step because failing to do so negatively impacts your ability to determine the best response methods and ways to meet your needs. It's important to remember that figuring out the problem and its impact is usually a relatively quick process in most cases. For instance, think about how long it would take to summarize the effect losing your job would have on your life; the impact a problem like that would have is immediately clear.

Another essential part of being response-focused is working with (instead of against) your emotions. Accept your feelings as they come and allow yourself to use them to help you effectively respond. It is so important to remember you don't get to choose your emotions, so denying their existence is unhelpful. Make space for whatever you feel because working through those emotions is essential in addressing the problem. Your feelings guide you, telling you things that help you better understand your needs, which helps you find solutions. For instance, using the earlier example of losing your job, you would probably feel anxious, worried, disappointed, and angry. Embracing and processing those emotions would help you take a response-focused approach.

Anxiety or worry is a sign that you need to do or say something (often both). Anxiety is a call to action; it grabs your attention to let you know you need to respond to something. In this case, the call to action would be to take steps to achieve the goal of finding a new job. It also helps you understand your needs in a particular situation. Feeling anxious about losing a job makes it clear that you need to find a new source of income to relieve the anxiety. When you respond to your anxiety, you can successfully meet your needs, dissipating that anxiety. Once you meet that need, there is no longer a reason to be anxious.

It is vital to note that effectively responding to anxiety requires you to confront the source of stress, not avoid it. People often use avoidance as a shortcut to anxiety relief. In the short term, avoidance provides temporary relief, but in the long run, avoidance fuels anxiety because the source of the anxiety continues to exist. You must confront and respond to the anxiety to get long-lasting relief.

The more you avoid, the worse the anxiety will get. For example, deciding not to look for another job because you feel overwhelmed would only lead to temporary relief. Although distracting yourself would help a little, the anxiety would continue growing because you ignored its call to action. You'd constantly be reminded that you still don't have a job, and if you chose to continue ignoring the stress, you'd keep needing to find new ways to engage in avoidance. If you avoided it for too long, you'd risk depression setting in because when we experience stress with no consistent relief, we are more likely to fall into a depressive state. Avoidance is not the solution to our problems because it doesn't even address the problem itself. Avoidance is failing to do what anxiety calls us to do, which is to respond through action.

Disappointment is a sign that you need to grieve something so you can heal, and healing is essential for your well-being. Anytime you experience loss, you need to grieve. We often associate grief with death, but grief can come from loss of any kind. Disappointment is an emotion that frequently happens after a loss, so when we experience it, it's usually a sign that we need to take the time to grieve.

Losing a job is a loss. Even if you hated the job, prematurely losing it would cause complicated feelings you must acknowledge and work through to emotionally and mentally recover. Pretending to be unbothered only delays the grieving process, making it more challenging to think clearly and respond effectively to the situation. To effectively grieve, take the following steps:

1. Acknowledge your pain and any other emotions you are experiencing.
2. Accept that loss can trigger many different and unexpected feelings and make space for them all without judgment.
3. Understand that your grieving process will be unique to you.
4. Seek face-to-face support from people who care about you.
5. Support yourself emotionally by taking care of yourself physically and mentally.

The chart below can help you recognize the difference between grief and depression.[19]

Grief	Depression
There is an identifiable loss	A specific loss may or may not be identified
The person's focus is on the loss	The person's focus is on the self
Fluctuating ability to feel pleasure	Inability to feel pleasure
Fluctuating physical symptoms	Prolonged and marked functional impairment
The closeness of others is usually comforting	Persistent isolation from others and self
Able to feel a wide range of emotions	Fixed emotions and feeling "stuck"
May express guilt over some aspects of the loss	Has generalized feelings of guilt
Self-esteem is usually preserved after the loss	Feelings of worthlessness & self-loathing are common

Managing a Secondary Emotion

Anger is unique and complex because it happens in response to other emotions, so you must identify your primary emotions when you feel angry. Anger, similar to anxiety, is a call to action. Specifically, it brings your attention to a "wrong" you desire to make right. It also happens in response to situations that make you feel other negative emotions, like losing your job. In the example of a job loss, the primary emotions that lead to anger are disappointment and anxiety.

To be clear, the shift from your primary emotions to anger often feels instantaneous. In other words, it usually feels like they hit you all at once because it all happens so quickly. But it's still necessary to recognize how they are connected so you can best understand and respond to the anger you feel.

Anger commands your attention so you can find healthy, effective solutions to your problems (i.e., seeking a new job, assertively and thoughtfully communicating your feelings about being fired, seeking information about why the decision was made, etc.). It is important to note that anger is not a call to be violent or abusive. Those responses occur when a person doesn't deeply understand the complexity of anger, doesn't take the appropriate time to process it, and struggles with emotion regulation. Violence and abuse only cause more problems (and more negative emotions), so they are not appropriate responses to anger.

An important call to action with anger is communication. Please note that you cannot make someone take accountability; you can only hold them accountable. When you express your feelings assertively and thoughtfully, you validate them and make others aware that they caused them. There is power and relief in holding others accountable for the pain they caused you. Of course, this will not always be possible or even the best decision in every situation. However, when you can, and when it's helpful and safe to do so, communicating your feelings to the person who caused them can be a valuable part of the healing process, even though it is not necessary. When this isn't the right choice or an option, thankfully, processing your feelings with yourself and others you trust still helps you heal over time.

Recognizing and working with all the feelings related to your anger helps you determine the best way to decrease (and often eliminate) the intense emotions caused by the problem. You can best process anger when you acknowledge the primary emotions that caused it. When you work with all your feelings, you can effectively respond to the situation, whereas if you only accept the anger, you are more likely to act out of rage. Processing the primary emotions, in addition to the anger, allows you to better understand what you feel so you can respond to the situation in a way that will meet all your needs. Of course, as always, it takes time to work through difficult emotions, even when you understand them. This is by no means a quick process.

Finally, once you have analyzed the problem and allowed yourself *adequate* time to process your feelings, you are ready to identify ways to respond and to determine how to implement your response effectively. Everything you did in the first two steps allows you to be in the best head space to respond to the problem.

In summary, the process of working from a response-focused mindset requires you to first accept that your choices determine most of the outcomes in your life, and even when life throws something unexpected your way, you still have some control because you choose how you respond.

Then, you analyze the problem, which allows you to identify the need the problem created. In the case of losing your job, your need is financial security and possibly regaining a sense of purpose, which work often provides. You simultaneously identify and process your emotions, allowing you to fully grasp the unfortunate event's impact and what it's calling you to do to meet your needs. Your feelings enable you to understand your needs better since one of their primary purposes is to guide you through your circumstances. Processing will take time and will need to be done frequently in order to work through the intensity of the emotions.

Depending on the situation, processing could take hours, days, weeks, or even months. The good news is that you do not have to wait until you have completely worked through your feelings before you can take action. If you are committed to and consistent with processing, you will gradually begin to feel more emotionally regulated because you are meeting your emotional needs. This will make it easier to start responding to the problem while you also continue to process and work through what you feel. It is even common to still process feelings *after* resolving a situation because solutions often take less time to implement compared to the time we may need to emotionally recover from what we went through. Plus, some of the emotional relief will come from the situation being resolved.

Lastly, once you have taken the previous steps, you are in the correct mindset to determine a course of action that will meet your needs and subsequently improve your emotional state further. When it comes to losing your job, that would include steps like these:

1. Update your resume and request references.
2. Research and apply for new jobs.
3. Reach out to your support network for job opportunities or recommendations.
4. Reach out to a loved one for emotional support and, if needed, financial support or temporary housing.
5. Find a job recruiter to work with so the process is less overwhelming.
6. Consider and possibly pursue a different career path with more stability and fulfillment (which, of course, would require you to make another plan using the response-focused method).
7. Pursue a job that you can acquire quickly as a temporary source of income as you work on finding another job that actually aligns with your career path.
8. Pursue entrepreneurship if that's your goal.

When you take these kinds of steps and *persistently* do everything in your control, you'll have positive outcomes in most situations.

Short-Term vs. Long-Term Distress

Sometimes, when we feel helpless, it's not because we don't have things we can do but because we don't like what the problem calls us to do. In other words, it's not that we don't know how to solve our problem, but we don't like what we need to do to improve our situation. For example, most of us know when we are in an unhealthy or stagnant relationship, but we *don't like* that this realization calls us to end the relationship altogether. Even after countless failed attempts to improve the relationship, we continue making whatever excuse we can to lead us away from the correct decision of going our separate ways.

That's the thing about free will. We get to choose what our decisions are based upon. Making decisions that are good for us and that genuinely respond to the problem, no matter how difficult or uncomfortable, is always best. However, we often choose to make decisions that seem less hard in the short term. We are frequently tempted by what feels easiest. Unfortunately, in a lot of situations, what feels easiest often deters us from choosing what is best for us and, ironically, ends up causing us more problems in the long run.

There is one emotion we have to be particularly aware of during our decision-making process. That emotion is hope. When we are making a decision, we must remain mindful of the type of hope our decision is based upon. Hope for how we wish things could be and hope informed by what seems most likely to happen based on our experiences in the situation are two very different types of hope. The first one is very appealing and can draw us further into a cycle that, in reality, doesn't seem to be improving. The latter is rational and sheds light on whether the situation is genuinely worth more time, effort, and patience or calls for a different response.

In situations where we are not the only one who determines the outcome, such as in relationships, we must be wary of hope based only on how we wish things could be. We must remember the only person we control is ourselves. This means when we are trying to resolve a situation in a way that also requires someone else's efforts, even if we do all we can, it still won't lead to change without that person's consent and participation. When they choose not to participate, we are forced to make a decision that *doesn't require* their participation if we want long-term relief from the distress and positive change.

An easy way to remember how much control you have over a situation is to divide one hundred percent by the number of people involved. So, if you are trying to make a monogamous relationship work, that means you only have fifty percent control since doing so requires the willingness and participation of two people. Humans have free will, and each individual is in charge of themselves. We can encourage and positively influence someone to use their power over themselves in a positive way, but we cannot *make* them do so. Because of this, even if you did everything in your power to improve the two-person dynamic, you still wouldn't be able to pass fifty percent. You also do not have any *direct* power over what someone else does with their share of the control.

You have to allow yourself to care more about the long-term results when *choosing* your responses to life's problems. I get it; the short-term result is very tempting. After all, it provides instant gratification, whether staying in a dissatisfying relationship because it has good moments or avoiding applying for a job because the search feels too overwhelming. Whatever the situation, doing what's best for the long term will ultimately lead to the best outcomes for you. The struggle involved in creating change and enduring some uncertainty is well worth it if it eventually leads to a better life—and a better you! Remember: you control your follow-up choices so you can continue to pursue what you desire for your life even after experiencing a loss.

If you find yourself stuck in a cycle where you've made multiple attempts to improve, you are eventually only left with choosing the hardest option. This decision will provide you with the change and relief you desperately need. The alternative would be choosing to continue in the cycle, but despite good moments, staying in an unhealthy relationship or ignoring the looming anxiety of unemployment causes you *chronic* distress.

When you have tried alternatives with no success, choosing the hardest choice *guarantees* change. This will cause distress too, but the difference is that *this* distress is temporary and will dissipate over time if you appropriately respond to your needs (and continue to make good decisions). A decision that effectively addresses an ongoing problem eventually relieves you of a cycle of chronic psychological distress. Inaction or continuing to make a decision that is not working keeps you in a cycle that can only be resolved by making a difficult choice.

Of course, there will be times when less difficult choices are successful. For instance, maybe you and your partner agree to go to therapy, and this ends up leading to consistent positive change that breaks the cycle. You won't always need to resort to the more challenging decision, but there will be times when circumstances consistently show you it would be the best choice. When that happens, it is up to you to accept this reality if you want to improve your life and end the cycle of chronic distress. You must accept what your attempts show you and what people's *patterns* of behavior tell you. If there is no change after implementing less difficult choices over a reasonable amount of time, you must shift to a different solution to your problem, no matter how difficult.

Ultimately, you must decide what matters more: choosing situations that provide you with wavering happiness and chronic distress or making decisions that will cause you temporary distress but also improve your life by ending the cycle and providing the opportunity for better choices going forward. Your free will enables you to choose either route, and there is no shame in either option. Even if other people disagree, you still get to decide how you respond to your life's problems. After all, it's your life, and you are in charge of how your story goes.

What I care about the most is that you understand the *why* behind your decision so you can be sure it's a consciously informed one made with your full awareness. I want you to fully internalize that if you choose the "easier" route, you do so because it feels more convenient and suitable for you at the time. I want you to internalize that you might be rejecting what the situation is calling you to do because that option requires more energy and feels scary. After all, it's uncharted territory (but if explored, it is a new path that will be charted by *your* choices). I want you to internalize that this decision is not because you aren't capable of pursuing the more difficult choice—because you are. You may need to make a plan and take steps before implementing the final decision so that you are putting yourself in the best position in the aftermath, but all of this is still an indicator of just how capable you are.

How you feel is not always an indicator of your true capabilities. Think about how often you've felt you couldn't do something, faced it anyway, and found you were capable. Whether learning to ride a bike, starting a new job, improving your self-esteem, taking a challenging class, or ending a relationship, feeling fear or any other negative emotion rarely means we aren't capable.

I want you to internalize that how you feel does not always indicate what's best; often, the best decision initially makes you feel the worst. Generally speaking, making a difficult choice usually doesn't evoke a bunch of positive feelings (at least not without some negative ones mixed in). You must consider other factors, like the outcomes of your attempts at change, to make a well-informed decision. If you rely *only* on how the decision makes you feel, you will often be misled. This is especially true when you choose to ignore what the negative emotions are *calling you to do*. Remember that many of your feelings are a call to action, so even though it doesn't make you feel good to think about doing what is hardest, those same negative emotions may be communicating that that's what needs to be done.

Again, choosing not to respond to the problem or avoiding the difficult choice when other attempts have failed is rightfully your decision to make. Just be sure you understand the *why* behind your choice, any long-term consequences, and whether your decision aligns with your long-term goals and needs.

Processing your decision is about being aware of the underlying reasons behind your choices. Being fully aware of the reasoning behind our decisions allows us to maintain an internal locus of control, which keeps us empowered and aware that we can make a different choice at any time. Suppose we don't accurately process how we arrived at our decision. In that case, we risk developing an external locus of control and feeling helpless (we will discuss this more in the next chapter). At the end of the day, being response-focused is simply about responding to the problem and deeply understanding your response, but how you decide to respond is up to you. It also involves identifying gradual steps you need to take in order to complete the full response to the problem. I hope you will eventually choose what is best for you in the long term, even though the short-term solution may be tempting. Ultimately, you will be so glad you did, despite what it took to get there.

CHAPTER 4

Avoid Helplessness

You have too much power to let it go to waste. Don't let your circumstances create the illusion that you are powerless.

ystemic racism, limited resources, social inequalities, and generational trauma all make achieving success and mental well-being incredibly challenging. But thankfully, our free will still gives us significant influence over how our lives unfold. Being self-aware, having an internal locus of control, and prioritizing our mental health help us improve our decision-making. It also decreases feelings of helplessness, which lowers our risk for mood disorders like chronic depression and anxiety.

As stated earlier, our emotions communicate things about our needs and often serve as a call to action. It's important to note that sadness and anxiety are normal emotional experiences; they cannot be avoided, but chronic mood disorders can be prevented. Of course, we can't, with one hundred percent certainty, avoid developing a mood disorder because there are many individual and societal factors.

However, we can protect ourselves by taking care of our emotional needs, processing our experiences, and responding effectively to situations that arise.

Learned helplessness is a mental state associated with depression that typically occurs after a person has had multiple negative experiences and now feels that trying to prevent future ones is pointless. Over time, they start to believe there is nothing they can do to stop negative experiences from happening. They feel as if their life is out of their control, making it challenging for them to find ways to improve their situation.

Of course, negative experiences are inevitable for us all. They are a part of life, just like positive and neutral experiences. No matter how hard we try, we will still sometimes feel frustration, disappointment, grief, and sadness. However, we can decrease our likelihood of developing learned helplessness by being mindful of our free will. In life, *some* of our negative experiences are due to, and can be improved by, our choices. This means making better choices can help us avoid unnecessary distress.

To better understand learned helplessness and how it affects us, we can look to one of the famous psychological studies that first discovered this phenomenon. Psychologists Dr. Martin Seligman and Dr. Steve Maier first discovered learned helplessness behavior in the 1960s.[20] They used dogs as their research subjects, and since we are also mammals, the results taught us a lot about ourselves as humans. Here is a quick breakdown of the two phases of the experiment. (Please note the first code of ethics for psychologists came out in 1953, so the rules around ethical research were new and less strict at the time of this study).

In phase one, researchers divided the dogs into two groups and placed them in chambers where they received mild electrical shocks. The only difference between the groups was whether they could do something to stop the shocks. The dogs in the "escape group" had a button in their chamber that they could press with their nose to stop or avoid the shocks. The dogs in the "non-escape group" could not escape the shocks, despite attempting to, because their chamber did not have a button.

In phase two, the two groups of dogs were placed in a box with a low divider they could easily step over. Now, all the dogs could easily escape the shocks simply by crossing the divider at any time. The purpose of phase two was to observe how their experiences in phase one would affect their behavior.

The researchers found most of the dogs from the non-escape group didn't even attempt to escape despite now being able to do so. It seemed their past unsuccessful attempts led them to give up even though their escape efforts in phase two would have been successful. In other words, they had developed learned helplessness. In comparison, most of the dogs from the phase one escape group quickly jumped the barrier to avoid being shocked. Their earlier experience of preventing shocks by performing a simple action helped them feel empowered during phase two. Because of this, they quickly problem-solved how to avoid the shocks again.

This experiment reveals how past experiences can influence current and future behavior. If we've had multiple adverse experiences and struggled to find solutions, we can become susceptible to learned helplessness. Considering the experiences of Black people in America and other parts of the world, it is easy to see how we may be more prone to learned helplessness. Many societal barriers have created challenges and impacted us psychologically. Just like in phase two of the experiment, there are ways to overcome these barriers, but that does not negate the fact that they often create a significant challenge and can lower our willpower. Because of this, we can begin to feel our efforts are in vain even when this is not the case.

Expectedly, trauma is a common cause of learned helplessness. Everyone experiences trauma, but millions of Black people have endured a heartbreaking amount. Plus, historical trauma from institutions like slavery and segregation still affects us today due to its generational psychological impact and the racist systems that still exist. The structure of our society indeed puts us at a higher risk. Still, by being aware, we can actively work against adopting this harmful mindset of learned helplessness, just as many of our ancestors did despite living through horrendous events.

One of the most important things to remember is that our personal experiences do not represent all possibilities. As humans, we rely heavily on our experiences to understand the world. It's easy to think our individual experiences are all there is because they're all we know, right? If all we know is what we've seen happen to us and our family and friends, that can easily become a template for what we believe is possible for us. After all, it can be hard to believe in something we haven't experienced directly. Cycles of generational trauma can often make it feel like this is just how things are and will continue to be.

Many of us grew up surrounded by adults battling learned helplessness (amongst other issues). Of course, this was not entirely their fault because the odds were against them, and many of them were in survival mode. It can be hard to believe you are capable of more when the world continuously says you aren't, your surroundings suggest the same, and trauma has generationally plagued the lives of your loved ones. It's hard to believe in something when you haven't seen it firsthand.

When I went out to the waiting room to greet my first Black therapy client after I completed my doctorate, she saw me, a dark-skinned Black woman who looked like her, and she couldn't hide the surprise on her face. In the world she had been exposed to, Black people weren't doctors, so seeing me was like seeing a unicorn. She had grown up in a Black neighborhood where having a graduate degree was uncommon and learned helplessness was the norm. At the time, she believed the biggest dream a Black person from her community could have was to play sports or work in the entertainment industry. Otherwise, you just did the best you could to get by. She was in her forties, and this was the first time she had a doctor who looked like her.

Once we began our therapy session, she told me, "I fear you won't understand the things I've been through because, clearly, you're a different kind of Black."

It often takes people a little time to warm up, so I appreciated her frankness. She was trying to find an explanation for how someone like her could become a doctor. For her, being a doctor was the White man's dream or, at the very least, only an option for "a different kind of Black" person. I had encountered this belief before with other Black clients and clients of color. Hell, I had also experienced it with White clients, who were just as surprised to see me simply because they stereotypically associated the word "doctor" with someone White too. But there I was. The Black unicorn. The Black doctor. I must be a "different kind of Black" to have gotten here.

I was sad to find out I was the first real-life example she had, but I was equally happy that we'd met. I was living proof that Black doctors existed. Of course, she had occasionally seen Black doctors in the media, but she had never been able to interact or converse with one. As we spoke more, it became clear that she began seeing other possibilities for Black people as more attainable, especially once I shared that I wasn't "a different kind of Black," as she had assumed.

I was a Black woman who had endured and worked through many difficulties she had also experienced, including these hardships:

- Sexual abuse and assault
- Parental divorce
- Insufficient emotional support during my upbringing
- Emotionally, psychologically, and physically abusive relationships
- Colorism

- History of diagnosed depression and anxiety disorders
- Black societal traumas, including racism and oppression

My client had assumed I had some miraculous life, and that's what she meant when she called me "a different kind of Black." She had assumed I'd enjoyed a very privileged upbringing. Also, when she saw my wedding ring, she thought my husband was White because she believed this type of success meant I didn't associate much with Black people or culture. In reality, my husband and all my closest friends are Black. Based on my career, she assumed I had to be so different from her, but we actually had a lot in common.

Here's the thing. I am not some unicorn who achieved an impossible feat. There are many successful and well-educated Black people in the world and within my family. I simply was someone committed to using my free will to try to create the best life for myself that I could, and I realized that doing so required me to take mental health seriously. I went to therapy to learn about my mental health and to start healing from my trauma so it would no longer determine the trajectory of my life. I also dedicated my life to self-work and pursuing self-growth by applying knowledge from psychology. Of course, all these things have taken hard work and conscious effort, but they are not impossible.

All Black people have experienced some form of trauma regardless of how privileged their lives might be. I wanted my client to understand that Black people can achieve and *have* achieved all kinds of success. Life can be challenging, and the impact of trauma is intense and multifaceted. Everyone's journey will have its hardships and hurdles along the way, but strengthening and caring for our relationship with ourselves gives us the best odds of overcoming them. Our relationship with ourselves *is* the foundation upon which everything else is built. We can't control the world around us or everything that life throws our way, but we do have control over whether we nurture our relationship with ourselves. We control whether we allow ourselves to acknowledge things we aren't proud of so we can begin changing them. We control whether we seek knowledge to help us grow from our current level of understanding and practice skills that help us become a better version of ourselves.

We all have two realities: the world and the world we interact with. The world we interact with is less than one percent of the entire world, but it can have a powerful influence over our beliefs and perspectives. Being told something, rather than experiencing it, has a very different impact on a person's reality. This, among many other reasons, is why positive Black representation, community events, and mentorship matter so much. Of course, we can believe in something even if we haven't experienced it firsthand (and many of us have done just that). However, just like seeing Santa Claus at the mall makes his existence seem more real to children, witnessing other Black people's significant accomplishments does the same for us. Our Blackness is indeed diverse, complex, and unique, but no matter our differences, we are all connected. There I was, Black like her, and I was a doctor.

Of course, we all desire our lives to go well. But even with examples of that possibility, remembering that we are in control can be hard at times, especially when we have struggled in the past. Those experiences can make us feel powerless or hopeless. We must protect and build our self-esteem and remain highly aware of what's in our control because, without conscious awareness and consistent practice, it's easy to fall into a problem-focused mindset instead of a response-focused one. Things won't always be easy, but it is essential to remember we are capable. When we take the time to explore the psychological impact of our experiences and practice effective problem-solving, we can protect our sense of control over our lives.

When we don't take enough time to self-reflect, we begin living on autopilot because our self-awareness decreases. Living this way makes us particularly susceptible to learned helplessness. It creates the illusion that things are just happening to us when, in reality, the vast majority of our life's outcomes are due to or can be improved by our choices. By staying mindful of how powerful our free will is, we can create a better life for ourselves. The following tips will help.

Maintaining a Capable Mindset

Be aware and beware of learned helplessness. Once you have a name for something, you can better monitor yourself for it. Here are some of the signs to look out for:

- Refusing to ask for help when you are experiencing a struggle
- Decreased motivation
- Often feeling out of control
- Living your life passively instead of actively living through deliberate, well-thought-out decisions
- Depressive symptoms
- Exhibiting signs of low self-esteem
- Believing your lack of success is due to a lack of ability
- Assuming success is solely dependent on factors outside of your control, such as luck

If you are experiencing many of these signs, you need to seek help and support. Learned helplessness can be very challenging to work through alone. Addressing any early signs of learned helplessness can prevent it from setting in as a mindset. Reach out to loved ones who can support you emotionally and help you problem-solve. Also, consider finding a therapist you connect with so they can help you figure out what situational, psychological, and emotional factors are contributing to this way of thinking. This will also allow you to work through any related trauma that could be part of the learned helplessness.

Remain mindful that there are usually multiple ways to respond to a problem. Consider which options will likely lead to the best outcomes and give you the most control over what happens next. When you find yourself in challenging situations, you want to determine ways to respond that will create positive change and give you the most control over future outcomes. As discussed in Chapter 3, being response-focused is the goal; this mindset is highly protective against learned helplessness.

A successful life requires getting comfortable doing things you don't want to do so you can get what you need. As stated earlier, one of the most significant barriers to change is when you aren't the biggest fan of the best solutions to your problems. When this happens, staying in the situation can seem simpler, but doing so ends up causing significant distress. The thing is, when we practice doing what we *need to do* over what we *want to do,* this usually leads to outcomes that give us *both* what we want and need. It's the difference between instant gratification and delayed gratification; what is instant isn't always the most fulfilling in the long run, and what takes the most effort and willpower often is.

People often fear change because they don't trust themselves to make good decisions. However, in most cases, it's not that we don't know a good decision from a bad one; it's that we fear the uncertainty that will come afterward. We wonder things like: *If I do move, will I be happy? What would my life look like without this person? Will I like this new job?* Of course, these types of concerns are entirely valid, but we often ask these questions without keeping in mind the level of control we have over what happens next. We create happiness, and change is a gift because it's an opportunity to do just that through making choices that improve our lives. Doing the same things leads to the same results, so change provides salvation from what is no longer working for us. All we have to do is continue to make healthy choices for ourselves after our initial decision and seek healthy guidance from others if we are struggling to figure it out on our own.

When making a decision that will lead to change, promise yourself that you will continue to do what's best going forward. If you commit to making good decisions, no matter how hard or uncomfortable, you will continue to have better outcomes.

Be sure to look inward. There's a reason why no matter who my therapy client is, I can always connect their current behaviors and thought patterns back to their past. This is because our experiences shape us. Our everyday thoughts and behaviors reflect what we've been through and what we've worked on or not worked on. When we want to change something about ourselves, it requires us to identify those connections and unlearn what needs to be unlearned. Self-reflection allows us to recognize our growth areas and the causes of certain behaviors. Once we understand these parts of ourselves, we can begin to work toward healing and unlearning. Doing so also helps us build self-trust and improve our decision-making, which can help us avoid preventable trauma.

Question what you have always deemed the norm and decide whether you desire something different. Ask yourself why you make the decisions you make, and try to process how your behaviors relate to your past experiences. Do any of your life choices remind you of someone else who chose to do the same? How did that work out for them, and do you desire a different outcome? What would you need to do differently to achieve that?

Ask yourself two questions every day: 1) What would the person I am trying to become do in this situation? and 2) What would the person I am trying to become think about this situation?

Keeping your answers to those two questions in mind helps you hold yourself accountable to work toward change. It is so easy to make excuses for your behaviors and thoughts. The problem is that continuously defining yourself by things you're trying to change makes it harder to progress. When opportunities present themselves, you want to ask yourself those two questions so you can take small steps toward the change you desire. Accountability truly is the key to growth.

In addition to reading up on psychology and possibly choosing to go to therapy, practice journaling and take note of behavioral patterns you see within yourself. Write them down to make yourself consciously aware, and create a plan to decrease the tendency of unwanted behaviors. What tends to trigger you or trip you up? What will you do differently in those circumstances, and how will you begin holding yourself accountable? How do you desire your life to be, and what would you need to do differently to achieve that?

Process your experiences by talking to yourself about them, but not in a judgmental way. You want to be curious and attempt to understand what happened and why. Being overly critical will cause shame and likely impede your ability to increase self-understanding.

Learn to differentiate between your intuition guiding you and your trauma misleading you. When you haven't yet connected the dots between how your experiences influence your current thoughts and behaviors, it creates the illusion that how you are is "just who you are." Unresolved trauma gets in the way of connecting with your authentic self. Trauma often influences you on more of a subconscious level and negatively impacts your decision-making. When you pretend these negative experiences didn't affect you, you allow your traumatized self to be in charge of your life. The only way to break this cycle is to increase self-awareness by exploring trauma's impact on you; doing so brings your unresolved trauma from your subconscious to your conscious awareness.

Pay attention to how your decisions relate to past mistakes. If your decisions are part of a repeated cycle that continues to lead to the same unwanted outcomes, then this is likely your trauma misguiding you. However, if your decision will break a behavioral pattern that has consistently failed you and is the result of you facing hard truths, then this is likely your intuition guiding you. Always listen to your intuition, as the voice of your trauma will only keep you from improving your life.

When you're working toward healing and unlearning, you must allow your healing self to be in charge. Doing so enables you to meet and become more of your authentic self, but emotional discomfort is a guaranteed part of the journey. Facing the effects of your trauma can feel very disruptive to your identity. You'll learn new things about yourself and discover parts of yourself that are trauma responses you need to unlearn. The healing journey requires you to remain open-minded and deeply explore who you are; it also requires you to face hard truths and heavy emotions. The only way to no longer allow your unresolved trauma to be in charge is to acknowledge it and explore how it has affected you emotionally, mentally, and behaviorally.

Consider possible (rational) outcomes before making a decision. Before taking action, you can usually predict what might happen. All you have to do is take a moment to think before acting. For instance, if you're considering having unprotected sex with a stranger, you can quickly determine the possible consequences of that decision. Go through each consequence (i.e., sexually transmitted diseases, unwanted pregnancy, possibly feeling used, etc.) and imagine yourself in each situation. Ask yourself how you would feel and what you would do if these things happened. How long would these consequences last, and are they worth the risk? Can you still have what you desire but also lower your risk? For instance, by choosing to use protection, you can still have sex while also significantly reducing your risk of unwanted outcomes. If, through your hypothetical processing, you determine the cons outweigh the pros, adjust your plans. If you still want to have sex, that's perfectly fine. However, making the simple choice of using protection can help you avoid serious negative consequences that may be devastating or life-altering.

Every choice you make has a consequence, good, bad, or neutral. Even something as simple as what you choose to eat for lunch has the neutral consequence of meaning you're unable to eat something else for lunch that day because you'll be full. It's important to remember life is not a video game; there are no do-overs, so when faced with a decision with clear possible negative consequences, you must take it very seriously.

There are times when you can be spontaneous with little to no risk. Decisions like where you go for your next vacation or what outfit you wear on a particular day don't necessarily require much thought or analysis. However, whenever you are presented with a more serious situation, you should take the time to think your decision through. Before making a choice, walk yourself through the *likely* consequences. Are they good? Are they bad? What are the odds of these things happening? Even if the odds are small, is the risk worth it?

If you decide to take a chance, ensure at least this one thing is true: the risk has the serious potential to benefit you over the long term and has limited negative consequences, which you're prepared to face. Go for that job. Pursue your dreams. Ask your crush out on a date. These types of risks are worth taking, but others may not be. It's up to you to think things through and decide what is best for your life.

Step outside your bubble as often as possible. Sometimes, problem-solving is difficult because you only seek information from same-minded people. Of course, this is not always bad. It only becomes an issue when you close your mind to other perspectives and reliable information. Getting different perspectives gives you more to consider, which is often very helpful for your growth. It is so important to step out of your bubble, speak to people different from you, and seek new experiences. You don't know what you don't know, and it is impossible to know everything. New ideas expose you to new possibilities, which might just be the answer to your problems.

Think about situations simply. How you process information determines your feelings. So, when you overcomplicate the solutions to your problems, you can unintentionally make them feel impossible to achieve. Thinking about your situation simplistically helps you work toward change. You don't want to overwhelm yourself before you even attempt to accomplish your goal. That would increase the likelihood of feeling automatically defeated and not working toward it. Instead, you'll feel more empowered when you make a simple plan with clear, gradual steps.

In creating a simple plan, you speak to yourself in a way that helps you feel confident and reassured about what you're trying to accomplish. Initially, writing *Bold. Black. & Becoming* felt like a massive project. However, I chose to speak to myself in a way that allowed me to think about achieving this goal in the most simplistic way possible. I told myself there are technically only two things a person needs to be able to write a book: to be educated on the subject they desire to write about and to know a language so they can write and read words. That's it, and thankfully, I have both of these abilities; therefore, I can write a book.

Of course, you could come up with more complicated ways of describing what it takes to write a book. However, choosing to speak to myself about it simplistically increased my motivation and self-efficacy. Thinking about your goals simplistically prepares you to face a challenge. Doing so is essentially a brain hack to help you when you possess the ability to tackle an important goal but are struggling with self-doubt. Simplistic thinking enables you to push forward.

Like all your emotions, self-doubt tries to communicate things to you. But your feelings are not foolproof; sometimes, they tell you things that aren't entirely accurate. Your emotions always matter, but sometimes, they're based on irrational thoughts or fears. If you have poor judgment in a situation, the feelings that result from that judgment will be misleading. You must have a deep, intimate relationship with your emotions so you can fully understand the thoughts that led to them and correct them when necessary.

Self-doubt and humility have a close relationship. Yes, you want to be humble, but you don't want to discount your abilities or lessen your belief in yourself. You need to remain mindful of a fine line between the two. You can achieve more if you're willing to make mistakes and apply what you learn from them. You also accomplish more when you are able to recognize the difference between a deficit in knowledge (which is something that can be sought out and acquired) and a deficit in ability. Most things that you believe you can't do have more to do with gaining knowledge first and practicing than they do your actual ability. For instance, I currently can't do a backflip, but with time, energy, education, and practice, I could absolutely learn how to. Just because you don't initially know how to do something doesn't mean you can't figure it out. Everything you currently know how to do began from a state of not knowing, but you learned, and you are still capable of learning more. Having a perfectionistic attitude keeps you from growing and reaching your full potential.

Develop this kind of attitude: "This makes me nervous and even a bit doubtful because the goal *feels* intimidating, but I am willing to try and figure it out. I am willing to see what I can do when I allow myself to invest patience, time, consistent effort, and self-encouragement. If, after all that, I find I cannot achieve my goal, I will seek a new one and take what I learned from the experience for my self-betterment. I will not allow the initial doubt to stop me from discovering my true capabilities."

Be willing to shift your perspective. Often, the solutions we seek can be found by permitting ourselves to see our situation through a new lens and allowing ourselves to consider other possibilities. Since our perspective (thoughts) impact our emotions and behaviors, processing our circumstances from a different point of view and being more cognitively flexible can reveal new insights. This can also happen by processing our problems with others who may be able to present us with solutions we hadn't yet thought of ourselves.

Since problems can naturally feel overwhelming, we can accidentally put ourselves in a helpless mindset without even realizing it. We are so disappointed by our circumstances, and the heaviness of those feelings can cause us to mistakenly believe that we are doomed.

Just like with the dogs in the second part of the experiment, we can sometimes have a fixed or limited mindset that prevents us from seeing alternative solutions that are right in front of us.

A great practice to adopt when you say you can't do something is to ask yourself why. Asking ourselves why forces us to analyze the reasoning behind the "can't." It helps us assess whether we genuinely *can't* do it or we can, but we would just need to plan and problem-solve beforehand to make it happen. Sometimes, we say we "can't" from an emotional place and not from a realistic one.

So, for instance, when I initially felt anxious about writing a book, if I had said, "I can't write a book," that would have been the anxiety speaking. Confronting myself with the "why" question would quickly reveal that to me. Sure, I needed to do a bit of research on the process, brainstorm the contents, outline the book chapters, hire an editor, etc., but that is not the same as not being able to do it. The "why" reveals that there are just steps that I need to do before and during the process. Through processing and planning, I absolutely can (and did) write a book.

There are many things that you have convinced yourself you "can't" do, but if you were willing to *honestly* ask and answer the whys, you will find that you can. It may take thought, time, stages, and dedication, but regardless, it is still something you can do if you are willing to plan accordingly.

Remember, words have meaning and energy, so we should use them with intention and thoughtfulness. We don't want to accidentally create mental blocks that prevent us from pursuing things that we are capable of accomplishing or that can improve our life circumstances. "Can't" is a word that should be reserved for things you genuinely *can't* do. Not things you are afraid to do or don't want to do or things that are entirely possible but would require preparation. If you say can't and, through the why, find that "can't" is not an accurate representation of the situation, correct yourself and replace the word to remain mindful that at any time, you can choose to change your mind. Instead, say, "I am anxious" or "I am confused about how to achieve this goal." This will also help you identify how you can tend to your needs and do what you can behaviorally to turn that "can't" into an actionable "can!"

Be sure to focus on the present, as it will help you feel less overwhelmed. Concentrate only on the step ahead of you. Of course, you know there are multiple steps, but be sure to place most of your energy on the step at hand. There will be plenty of time to focus on the next step when you get there. By disciplining your mind this way, you ensure that each step gets the adequate time and focus it needs, which increases the likelihood of success. Your mind will wander, which is normal; it's part of the journey, but remain in charge by choosing your focus.

Don't focus on the next task until you get there. Acknowledge, process, and release thoughts about future steps. You'll address relevant thoughts during the appropriate stages of achieving your goal, so there's no need to feed them a lot of energy beforehand. If, through your occasional mental wandering, you stumble across valuable insights for future steps, write them down so you can reference them at a later time. This will help you feel more mentally at peace because you have a record you can refer back to, and it will allow you to stay more present-focused. Redirect yourself as often as needed, and each time you do, you help yourself refocus on the step at hand. Be sure to redirect yourself with kindness and not criticism. Our brains are always thinking, so it is natural for our minds to wander. Accept it as part of the human experience, and lovingly talk yourself back to the task at hand.

I'm not trying to suggest that changing tendencies of learned helplessness is easy. However, I want you to realize your full potential and ability to protect yourself, regardless of your circumstances. Doing self-work takes tremendous dedication, and admitting your areas of growth takes humility and self-compassion. None of this happens overnight or quickly. Your response might require you to take time to make a plan or complete it in smaller steps. However, the point is that there is always something you can do to meet your needs and improve your situation. If it will lead to a better life for you and has little to no negative consequences, then it is likely the best decision.

Black people are capable of whatever we put our minds to, just like anybody else. We may have more to overcome in some ways, but this does not make us less capable. Learned helplessness can thankfully be unlearned; the first step is just being informed about it so you can protect yourself from it. If you need further inspiration, remember to look outside your small world. Many Black people have come a long way. Seek and surround yourself with people who are either working toward or have already achieved things you desire—especially people who may have a similar story to yours and have accomplished something you want to accomplish. If you cannot directly connect, indirect sources, such as reading their books or learning about them online, can be equally inspirational. You just have to remind yourself that their achievements represent what's possible if you're willing to work toward it.

Remember to dream big, make good choices, and seek information (and help when needed). Doing so keeps you empowered! Even when you don't feel it, know that you are capable and can create a better life for yourself.

CHAPTER 5

Corrective Experiences

Don't spend life limiting yourself.
Be uncomfortable and seek growth.

A corrective experience is a life event that profoundly changes our understanding of ourselves or others. These moments are transformative and create new meaning. They help us challenge our beliefs about ourselves and the world around us. In other words, they are a key component of our self-growth.

Corrective experiences are essential for everyone. The best thing about these experiences is that we can actively seek them out by challenging ourselves to do things differently, like facing a fear or changing a behavior. They can also happen organically; life circumstances can lead to a corrective experience even when we aren't seeking it. When this occurs, it's usually an experience we need even though we don't know we need it. Those are some of the best moments despite how emotionally challenging they can be.

I had an unexpected corrective experience as I was writing *Bold. Black. & Becoming*. I initially assumed I was mentally prepared. After all, as a clinical psychologist with years of experience, I am professionally qualified to share information on mental health. I'm a Black woman, which gives me unique qualifications to discuss Black mental health and experiences. I practice what I preach and have been dedicated to my self-growth for over a decade now. I seek to be better every day and push myself to do things, no matter how difficult, if I know they will contribute positively to my self-growth. With all that in mind, it felt like a safe assumption that I had everything I needed. But writing this book shed light on an unhealed wound I thought was fully healed, which led to another unexpected corrective experience.

Here's how it all went down. After months of endless writing, I unexpectedly had weeks of writer's block and was consumed with self-doubt. Although I had already confidently written ninety-five percent of the book, I suddenly felt unprepared to put on the final touches. How did I go from effortlessly writing to feeling so stuck and unmotivated at the end?

One morning, I sat at the dining room table in my home, which is where this book was born, and I stared at the blinking cursor, feeling uninspired. While I struggled to find the words to write, my husband happened to come downstairs. "Hey, baby! How is writing going?" he asked.

A heaviness grew in my chest from the weight of that question. Such a simple question, yet so triggering because it wasn't "going." I was stuck, and I felt defeated. I burst into tears and ran to embrace him at the bottom of the stairs.

Ironically, that question helped me tap into what was subconsciously burdening me. Through my sobs, I took a few deep breaths and said, "I'm just so afraid that people . . . other Black people . . . won't like my book. This weird part of me feels like I don't have the right to talk about these things even though I'm Black."

My husband began his response by showing empathy, making me feel validated and unjudged. Then, with so much sincerity and with words as poetic as Sojourner Truth's "Ain't I a Woman?" he said, "Baby, aren't you a Black woman in America? Aren't you a Black psychologist? Aren't you Black? *You* are exactly who should be speaking about these topics. You don't need anyone's validation or permission. We need and are looking for someone like you to be a voice that helps all of us. You already do that as a psychologist with your clients, and now you're writing this book to do it on an even larger scale. You're doing exactly what you're meant to do, and that is all the permission you will ever need."

He then reminded me of how my feelings related to my experiences with bullying. At that moment, it all clicked! That realization was my corrective experience. I realized being bullied by other Black kids during my childhood and adolescence still haunted me. I had been bullied for my dark skin, for "talking White," for getting good grades, and for not being "thick" enough. I didn't initially connect the dots because I'd already worked through the residual effects of this trauma in other ways. For so long, I'd questioned if I could wear clothing with messages related to Blackness. Not because I didn't know I was Black but because I subconsciously felt that I wasn't "Black enough" due to those experiences. However, I'd worked through those feelings.

Early in my adulthood, I realized the people who hurt me were hurting too. Their bullying behaviors were a product of their trauma; the painful messages they sent were about their struggles with self-love and had nothing to do with me. By the time I sat down to write this book, I had done a lot of self-work to heal from those experiences, so I didn't realize they were still affecting me. However, my writer's block revealed I had more healing to do because this new situation brought these feelings up in a unique way. I realized some small part of me still felt like I wasn't Black enough, despite how connected and confident I now felt as a Black woman.

Before this corrective experience, I had many others that led me to believe this trauma was entirely resolved. Those other corrective events taught me that my Blackness isn't defined by anything other than my existence and that there is no "wrong" way to be Black. My Blackness is a result of my Black parents and my Black American and Black Caribbean heritage. I may have some similarities with other Black people, but my Blackness also uniquely manifests because, regardless of our shared identity, I am the only me.

Through my other corrective experiences, I'd realized and accepted truths similar to the ones my husband had shared in that moment. However, the unique circumstances of writing a book had caused doubts to arise in the form of intrusive thoughts despite the fact that I had come so far in healing my relationship with my Black identity. See, that's the thing about trauma: as we continue to live our lives, new experiences will also present new opportunities to either further heal or not. The choice is ours and depends on our willingness to take that experience, process what it is revealing about us, and use it to grow.

It doesn't mean that the healing we did before wasn't "enough." Instead, it represents the beauty of the growth journey: *it is endless if we allow it to be.* We have to decide to commit to growing as much as we can in our lifetime and see moments like this as an opportunity to keep leveling up. At that time, I had mistakenly believed that all traumas could be entirely resolved. However, the reality is that profound traumas from our past, especially ones that impacted our identity development, have the ongoing potential to present new healing opportunities in our future.

As we continue through our lives, new challenges that are related to past hurts will come up, but with each level of healing and resulting corrective experience, we continue to move through these challenges with more and more efficiency. In other words, each level of healing we have already achieved becomes the foundation that helps us move through the next time even better. This allows us to keep evolving and multiply our healing by applying what we learned from each experience. The growth you have done thus far is yours regardless of what else life brings, but how much you *continue* to grow is dependent on how you respond when the next opportunity presents itself to you.

In that moment, I chose to respond by being honest and vulnerable with a safe person, which allowed me to progress to the next level of healing this wound. I am also looking forward to the next experience that will help me level up even more. I am now so grateful for that moment because it gave me another corrective experience that I didn't even realize I needed and that I am better because of. It was a reminder that feeling "Black enough" depends on me remaining mindful of what I have already learned through my experiences. I had long realized that, in the past, I had internalized the voices of those bullies, and over time, their voices had become my voice. Even though I had largely abandoned their voice, this experience was a reminder to stay vigilant because old wounds can sometimes try to find new ways to trip you up, even after you have healed in many ways. This corrective experience was a refresher of the lessons I had already learned so I can remember to apply them whenever needed. At that moment, I *recommitted* to living unapologetically Black so I could continuously heal and remain connected to myself. Because, after all, I am and *always have been* Black (and Black enough).

Your Corrective Experience

My corrective experience highlights some important points to remember about these events. Let's dive into them.

One traumatic event can mentally impact you in many ways, so there may still be more healing that needs to happen. The fact that something happened long ago and you processed it doesn't mean you won't need to address it again. You may want to move past trauma quickly, but when you do that, you fail to allow yourself to heal correctly. A good rule to follow is that the more significant the event, the more you will need to work through it in different ways at different times throughout your life.

There is no such thing as being completely "healed." The goal is to choose to live a lifestyle where you are committed to being in an ongoing state of *healing*. The process of healing requires maintenance and intentional action. We have to accept that we will need to reprocess certain experiences from time to time, which allows us to remain in a healing state. Healing is not about being void of emotion because that's not how the brain works. Instead, healing is about tending to your wounds and needs whenever necessary so you can continue to progress to the next level of your healing journey.

When we reprocess events, it allows the emotions that are attached to them to evolve, which in turn changes how we experience them. Each time we intentionally reprocess to deepen our understanding of what occurred and how it impacted us, we release painful energy through the release of emotion. Reprocessing is about maintenance and release. It allows the feelings to go from their original raw, intense state to new, graduated forms that feel more manageable despite the pain. Since we have processed it multiple times, we are already aware of the pain the experience caused, and by becoming deeply acquainted, we are impacted differently because we are doing the work to evolve in our healing.

Sure, you can quickly work through some upsetting events, like if someone spills your drink or cuts you off in traffic, but trauma is not something one simply "gets over." Traumatic experiences are like a gaping wound in your soul that requires time, patience, nurturing, vulnerability, self-awareness, and love to heal. And just like any major wound, once it's healed, you're left with a scar that you occasionally need to monitor and tend to. There is no quick fix for trauma, and pretending like something didn't affect you only allows it to control your life. Suppressing your trauma gives it control over you, and it will continuously show up in your relationships with others and your relationship with yourself until you do the work to heal the wound.

It is essential to be honest with yourself when you're bothered or hurt by something, even if you wish you weren't affected by it. Be sure to own your feelings, even if you think it's silly to feel how you feel so that you can work through them. As a human, you don't get to choose your feelings; you only decide whether you tend to them when they occur. Tending to them will always be the right choice because suppression just allows them to pile up and take over.

Life transitions are a common cause of emotions and thoughts resurfacing from past traumatic experiences. Thoroughly exploring these feelings and thoughts can further heal wounds and prevent you from accidentally repeating cycles of trauma. For example, for many people (including myself), their childhood trauma causes a lot of emotion to resurface once they become parents themselves. Remember: trauma impacts our lives in a powerful and multifaceted way, so you don't want to mistakenly believe one corrective experience is enough to understand its effect on you.

You must remain open and aware. This allows you to pick up on emotional cues from yourself that shed light on wounds that need healing and scars that require attention. If you feel stuck in a pattern, it may be related to your trauma. Self-exploration and self-reflection can help you uncover what you need to unlearn and process. They can also help you identify corrective experiences to seek out so you can continue to grow. For me, it was writing this book to further connect with my Blackness. For you, it will be something else. You must continue to peel back the layers, heal what needs to be healed, and *lovingly* push yourself to reach your full potential by facing your fears and insecurities.

Ruminating and processing are not the same thing. We want to be mindful not to mistake rumination for processing. When we ruminate, we are just going over the details of what occurred without our thinking having clear intent or purpose. This can cause unnecessary distress and delay the healing process. On the other hand, processing and reprocessing are done with purpose and intention; doing so is meant to benefit us and our mental health positively. The main difference is that processing not only explores the details of the events but analyzes the impact the event had on us mentally, emotionally, and physically. When we process, we ask ourselves questions like

- What was I thinking or feeling when that occurred? In comparison, what am I thinking and feeling now?
- What changes have I seen in myself in the aftermath of this event (good, bad, and neutral)? – This question also helps identify potential trauma responses to unlearn
- How do I feel about my relationship with this person now? Do I still desire a relationship with them?
- Did this have any impact on my core beliefs about myself?
- What do I need to do and say in order to help my healing process?
- When I analyze my behaviors and chosen thoughts, is there anything I need to remain mindful of or work on going forward to help me continue to grow?
- Did this experience impact my relationship with my body? If so, in what ways? What can I do to help myself repair my relationship with my physical self (if needed)?

Processing and reprocessing are about seeking wisdom and healing from what we experience. They help us identify what we need, what we can learn, and what we should do. Rumination is just fixating on what happened but not going any further. Processing takes things to the next level, and by going beyond the details of the event, we gain clarity that we can use going forward to help us care for and become better managers of ourselves.

When you say something aloud, especially with someone you trust, it loses some of its power over you. Failing to acknowledge and address your fears or insecurities allows them to become a mental prison that controls your life. Admitting them aloud takes a lot of vulnerability, but when you do, you can begin to challenge them. This is how you work toward growth. When you process them, you can also identify corrective experiences that can help you face the fears you want to overcome and gradually build confidence.

In therapy, we use exposure to help people overcome fears, such as social anxiety or a fear of dogs. Exposure is a type of corrective experience. Of course, exposure can be highly uncomfortable in the beginning stages, but it's also how we work toward positive change. Any fear you want to overcome requires exposure. After all, how can you work on improving something by constantly avoiding it? You can't. How do you get better at something without practice? You don't. For example, if you have social anxiety (which I used to struggle with, so I know how challenging it can be), your fear will grow if you constantly avoid social situations. Avoidance deprives you of opportunities to challenge your insecurities, improve your communication, and practice building your confidence. It denies you opportunities to build these skills and decrease your anxiety.

Sure, avoidance is easier, but its consequences can be devastating because it dooms you to deal with the same problems without any improvement. Think about it. Wouldn't working to overcome the fear so you no longer have to deal with it be easier than living with it for the rest of your life? When you look at the big picture, avoidance is a lot harder in the long run. Avoidance prevents you from getting more comfortable and increases your anxiety over time because the longer we go without corrective experiences, the worse our symptoms become.

In comparison, exposure helps you become desensitized to fear over time and allows you to learn and practice skills that help you better manage these symptoms. Social anxiety is something all humans experience to varying degrees and frequencies, and both of those differences largely depend on the current skill set that the individual has to help them work through the emotion. I still experience social anxiety occasionally (because I am human, and it's normal). Still, I now have skills that help me work through it so it isn't debilitating, and from each experience, I am able to hone these skills further. This allows me to get continuously better at managing and working *with* anxiety when it does occur (instead of fighting *against* it). Because whether I like it or not, it is an emotion, and it will occur throughout my life, so I either learn how to work with it or continue to suffer from it.

Let's use one more common example, the fear of flying, to further emphasize how this works. What happens if you have this fear and continue to avoid planes? The fear grows, and your mind continues to create more fear-driven thoughts, some irrational, causing the anxiety to worsen over time. In this case, your thoughts create a mental prison that impacts your behaviors, which causes you to avoid more. This produces a never-ending cycle of increasing anxiety and avoidance behavior. Instead of living in reality and responding to what happens, avoidance causes you to live in your head because your emotions result from the story you are creating in your mind and not your actual experiences. Anxiety and avoidance disconnect you from your *lived* experiences and cause you to live in the land of what-ifs (in your mind), which ultimately causes you to have less lived experiences altogether. Again, this is the vicious cycle that we must choose to break.

To be clear, this does not mean your feelings aren't valid or that the fear isn't real. Your fears matter, but you also deserve not to be limited by them if there is reasonable evidence that they are unlikely to happen. For example, you should be wary of walking down a dark alley at night or approaching a bear in the woods. Those are *very* reasonable fears to have, and avoiding these situations would demonstrate sound judgment.

Commercial flying, however, is the safest way to travel. Look at the facts. In 2022, over 853 million passengers safely flew in or from the U.S. alone. Worldwide, there are about 100,000 flights per day and 22.2 million per year, and they *all* safely reach their destinations. Because of how safe flying is (based on the statistics), it would take over 10 million flights before a person would be statistically at risk of a fatal injury, which is impossible to do in a lifetime. (This is just about odds based on statistical probability, so that also means a person could take 10 million flights, even though that's impossible, and still be completely fine!) [21]

The odds of a fatal plane crash are 1 in 11 million (0.01% for every 100,000 flights), which is extremely rare, and in general, plane crashes have a 95.7% survival rate for passengers. To put this into perspective further, your odds of being struck by lightning are 1 in 1 million, making it way more likely to happen. (Plus, 90% of people struck by lightning survive, which is still great odds, but the survival odds for a plane crash are still higher and way less likely to occur! Which means lightning is statistically more life-threatening than planes.) [22]

Now, of course, a person has every right to continue to allow their fear to stop them from flying. After all, every person has the right to make their own choices for their life and to decide which fears they allow to dictate their decisions. But if someone wanted to overcome this fear, they would need to engage in exposure and gather facts, like the ones I shared, to help them lessen their anxiety. The first flight would be the hardest, but after safely reaching their destination, they would have evidence that their anxiety was lying to them about what would happen. With each flight, they would continue to gain corrective experiences that showed them everything was okay and their thoughts did not represent what would occur.

The initial emotional discomfort would pay off because it would lead to corrective experiences that decrease the fear over time. Before they know it, they could become an avid traveler who flies worldwide to have new experiences; avoidance could never allow them to grow in such a way. Most frequent fliers (including myself) started with a significant fear of flying, but with each *internalized* corrective experience, that fear began to significantly decrease and even dissipate. If anxiety and fear were a plant, avoidance would be the water that keeps it alive. When you avoid your fear, you miss out on corrective experiences that could help you work through it or, at the very least, emotionally regulate it so it's no longer debilitating.

The most important thing to remember is that when you have corrective experiences, you must process and internalize them. Here's a metaphor to help you remember how internalization works. Imagine that every time you have a corrective experience, liquid is added to a cup; the cup represents the mentality you want to heal from or overcome. As the cup fills, you get closer to achieving the goal you set out to accomplish through having the corrective experiences. But each time you don't fully process and internalize your corrective experiences, your cup gets punctured with a hole. That hole causes the liquid (the corrective experiences) to spill out, so despite having the experiences, you don't get closer to your goal. When you don't internalize them, you don't experience the long-term benefits of having them. However, when you do internalize them, any existing holes in the cup are patched up, and you can add more liquid (experiences). The more internalized corrective experiences you have, the closer you get to your goal, and eventually, you reach it!

When you've had a fear for a long time, it takes time for your nervous system to get the message that you no longer need to fear that thing or can, at the very least, fear it a lot less. You must remind your brain of what actually happened and do so each time the fear returns. Anxiety works like an accusation in a court of law. You have to present evidence to dispute it, and lived experiences are the best evidence there is. Your thoughts strongly influence your emotions and behaviors, so you must first change how you speak to yourself.

You help your brain shift its reaction by repeatedly talking to yourself about what happened and reflecting on the experiences you had in contrast to those you were fearful of having. When you don't do this, you fail to benefit from your corrective experiences. It is not enough to just have the experiences. You also have to internalize them through purposeful conversation with yourself and others, which helps recondition your nervous system and update your beliefs. If you continue to scare yourself with what-ifs and don't intentionally shift your mindset, you don't get the benefit from the corrective events.

When it comes to what-ifs, remember they're questions, and you should treat them accordingly. When your mind throws a what-if your way, answer it. How would you handle that situation? What would you do? What's the likelihood of it happening in the first place? What is the most likely outcome? Is worrying about it even worth your energy, and is your train of thought rational? Gather any necessary information and make a plan. Talk yourself through what's in your control and how you would respond to the situation.

Constantly asking a bunch of what-if questions with no response causes you to feel powerless and scared. By answering the questions, you move from feeling helpless to feeling self-assured. You also interrupt the endless stream of anxiety-provoking questions that are often unhelpful and sometimes irrational. Oh, and don't forget the power of saying "no" to yourself to shut down unhealthy or distressing thoughts. Intrusive thoughts are part of the human experience, but you still control how you respond to them. Don't fuel intrusive thoughts by treating them as fact. Acknowledge them, talk yourself through them by focusing on what's in your control and identifying ways to respond, remind yourself of previous corrective experiences that relate to the situation, and allow the thought to pass.

I hope you will only choose to feed the fears that serve you, and I hope you will seek corrective experiences to overcome the ones that keep you from the life you desire.

You must have a rational perspective when it comes to your corrective experiences. It's easy to fall into the trap of continuing to justify a fear with questionable evidence. Since the fear can feel protective, you can unintentionally fuel your unreasonable fear. For example, I could have allowed my experiences of being bullied in high school to justify avoiding forming friendships with Black women. But it would have been unfair, misguided, and limiting to let those few people prevent me from having something I truly desired. Thankfully, I realized those girls who bullied me were not representative of all Black girls, and I currently have many close friendships with Black women.

Since our thoughts impact our behaviors, we can sometimes accidentally cause our beliefs to come true. I elaborate on this in the next chapter, but for now, remember that if we genuinely want to get the most out of our corrective experiences, we must be open-minded, non-defensive, self-reflective, and willing to have our beliefs challenged and to take in new information.

Self-discovery is one of our primary purposes in life, but not everyone experiences an upbringing that genuinely supports this goal. As discussed throughout this book, trauma and other events can disrupt our connection with our authentic selves. One of the most common causes of this disruption is the quality of parent-child relationships. Because of expectations and beliefs, many parents mistakenly *tell* their children who they are instead of allowing them the freedom to discover themselves. Even loving parents with strong opinions can fall into the trap of telling their children who they should be based on culture, gender, and other factors. If this wasn't the case, I wonder how many more women would be mechanics, love video games and fishing, and choose not to have children. I wonder how many more men would be childcare workers and love baking and self-care activities like pedicures and massages. I wonder how much more beautiful diversity, individuality, and authentic self-expression we would see across the board if, from birth, people weren't made to feel they had to be a certain way to be accepted or considered "normal."

The human experience is highly complex, and an "ideal" life depends on the individual. Just like you're trying to get to know yourself, other people are trying to get to know themselves too. It's a personal journey, and the lack of a safe space for self-exploration disrupts the process. We are unique individuals who must look *within* to discover ourselves. When it comes to self-discovery, living a life based on conditioning causes a major disconnect from our authentic selves. We don't all want or like the same things, and that's how it's supposed to be, so be sure to make space to discover who you are independent of anyone's expectations. Don't allow other people to convince you that *their* ideal life is yours. We are all on uniquely separate journeys, and many of those people who are pressuring you aren't even living authentically themselves. Conformity of self-expression does not allow for authenticity; your true self lies within your individuality, and you deserve to be celebrated for who you truly are.

Seek corrective experiences as frequently as possible. By the time you reach adulthood, most of your beliefs have come from other people telling you what to believe. Because of this, your beliefs are not your own unless you have genuinely explored them for yourself. They might feel like yours, but it's mainly because you've held them for so long.

Self-discovery, when done correctly and taken seriously, is a life-long journey. If you sincerely want to know *your* genuine opinions, likes, and dislikes, you must be curious and open to new information, especially when it challenges what you currently believe. You can learn a lot about yourself and others through the study of subjects like psychology, the human brain, history, and various sciences. In addition to books, documentaries are an excellent source of new information. By considering ideas with an open mind, conversing with people with different perspectives and experiences, and gathering *credible* information (always remember to fact-check), you can continue to evolve!

New information and experiences are not a threat; they are a gift! They help broaden and change your perspectives, further enlightening you and making you wiser. Just because you've believed something for a long time doesn't mean you should be close-minded or unwilling to have your beliefs change. The longevity of a belief does not guarantee accuracy or imply that you are "right." As human beings, we have a long history of believing the wrong ideas simply because we don't fully understand them yet. After all, endless people have believed in racism, genocide, homophobia, and other horrible ideas for centuries (and many unfortunately still do), but taking the time to educate ourselves reveals that these beliefs are misguided.

Here are some other examples:

- In the 1850s, there was a widespread belief that traveling by train would damage your brain and cause insanity because of all the rocking movement.
- People used to think it was absurd to believe planes could fly.
- From the 1970s until his death in 1995, Dr. John Yudkin tried to warn the world about the dangers of refined sugar and its damaging effects on the human body, but he was constantly ridiculed. Despite the fact that he was absolutely right!
- In the 1950s, people believed car seatbelts were annoying and unnecessary, and many chose to cut them out of their cars. Seatbelts didn't become mandatory until the late 1980s, despite the rates of fatal car crashes without them.
- Slavery was legal and widely accepted in the U.S. from 1619 to 1865. Racial segregation was legal and widely accepted from 1849 to 1950. This oppression happened for over 300 years because of strongly held beliefs that people were unwilling to change. Let that sink in.

The point is that the mentally healthiest people care more about being informed than being right about their current beliefs. They are sincerely open to being contradicted and finding out their original opinions were misinformed at any time. I believed some ideas (about myself and others) for many years, but through exploration and education, I no longer believe them.

It would be naïve to think our current level of understanding is all there is to know because life is too complex for that to be true. We are constantly learning new information about humans, the Earth, outer space, and other subjects, so it makes sense that our beliefs will change if we allow them to. Become consciously invested in seeking corrective experiences and new information, and see how your understanding of the world changes over time. I'm sure you'll enjoy seeing who you become when you abandon limiting beliefs and allow yourself to be endlessly interested in the world around you.

I hope understanding the power of corrective experiences will motivate you to face your fears and step outside your comfort zone. If corrective experiences teach us anything, they show us just how powerful our thoughts are and that our beliefs can sometimes create a mental prison that limits us. If we are unwilling to challenge our beliefs or seek new experiences, we unintentionally limit all we can get from life and sometimes even hurt others because of our ignorance. New information from *credible* sources only adds to our understanding of ourselves and the world. Sharing ideas and engaging in intellectual conversations allows us to grow and better understand each other.

We must decide what's most important: being "right" or being well-informed. When we value being informed more than being right, we learn so much. Human nature can sometimes cause us to get in our own way. We aren't perfect and don't know everything, so we must remain self-reflective to identify our biases (which we all have) and live life as students eager to learn. We are all beautifully different, and our primary job is to discover who we truly are because that will lead to our most fulfilling life and benefit everyone around us.

If you haven't already, I hope you will begin to fall in love with corrective experiences (as well as continual education and critical thinking). Once I learned about their power, value, and benefits, I became dedicated to seeking as many of them as possible, and I hope you will too! You deserve to know yourself intimately, live your truth, and keep evolving into better versions of yourself. Life is too short to spend it any other way.

CHAPTER 6

Trauma Responses

*Unlearning is how we get in
touch with our authentic selves.*

In *Healing Trauma*, Dr. Peter Levine writes, "Although humans rarely die from trauma, if we do not resolve it, our lives can be severely diminished by its effects. Some people have even described this situation as a "living death.""[23] This powerful quote summarizes just how imperative doing trauma work is if we want to live the life we were intended to live. Neglecting to do it is us unintentionally choosing to live a misguided, unfulfilling life that is almost like not living at all.

The first time someone asked me what going to therapy was like, I told them it was like meeting a stranger in the most unexpected but beautiful way. It was life-altering to discover that many of the traits I believed to be part of my true self resulted from my *unresolved* trauma. So far, my journey of self-discovery and healing has led to many big and small realizations. For example, for the longest time,

I hated wearing bright colors; I had assumed it just wasn't my thing. However, through therapy, I consciously recalled that this hadn't always been the case, so where did this aversion come from?

While reflecting on my childhood in therapy, I realized my preference for wearing darker colors began when I was bullied at school. By this time, I was already aware of the noticeable impact the bullying had on my confidence, but I hadn't realized its subtle, subconscious effects on my color preferences. Dark colors were less attention-grabbing, and I wore them because I felt insecure and wanted to stand out less. It turned out that being bullied had not only affected my self-esteem but also altered my behaviors and choices. I was shocked to realize that despite all the major progress I had made in rebuilding my confidence, I hadn't uncovered this *subtle* trauma response over the decade since those events had occurred. In all that time, I hadn't been fully aware of the *overall* impact of what I'd gone through.

Since the bullying began in my formative years, I had mistakenly believed this preference for dark colors was part of my authentic self. At the time, this seemed like a safe assumption because some people genuinely love wearing dark colors, and it has nothing to do with their trauma. But in my case, this choice wasn't as innocent as it had seemed; it began in response to deep pain and hurtful experiences. I'm sure this trauma response was, to some degree, helpful to my survival at the time. Like most trauma responses we develop, this behavioral change served the purpose of protecting me. There were probably many days I avoided additional traumatic experiences by blending in, and of course, this slowly reinforced the habit of wearing dark colors. Before I knew it, I believed I didn't like bright colors, and technically, this was true, but not for the reasons I'd assumed.

Once therapy helped me reveal the reason behind this decision, my attitude toward my personal preference changed. I didn't like that these bullies still had any influence over my life. I wanted *all* my power back, so I became intentional about healing this leftover wound. I experimented with wearing bright colors. At first, it felt uncomfortable because it didn't feel like "me," but I repeatedly reminded myself this discomfort was part of the trauma response. I had to wear bright colors to overcome the *learned* discomfort my trauma had caused. If I wanted to know how I genuinely felt about bright colors, I had to allow myself to get used to them again. I had to go through this unlearning process, and I had to continue building my confidence since this preference initially resulted from insecurities created by the bullying.

If I had *actually* preferred dark colors, that would have remained true after my healing process, but that's not what happened. Don't get me wrong, I still like them, but healing allowed me to rediscover a much stronger love for bright colors. When I wear bright colors, I now feel empowered, not just because of the trauma I worked through but because the colors match my authentic self! Thinking back, I realized I had once liked bright colors *a lot*. It wasn't until I began feeling insecure that this changed. The bullying had transformed me from an extroverted, secure, and outgoing person to someone who wanted to hide. Rebuilding my confidence hadn't revealed this connection because I had long since accepted this dark-color preference as part of my true self. It wasn't until I challenged and unlearned this trauma response that I reconnected with a piece of myself I had long abandoned and strongly desired to reclaim.

Sure, I could have lived a good life believing my preference for wearing dark colors was innocently rooted in my self-discovery and not my trauma. However, realizing its true origins allowed me to heal from a trauma response that had subconsciously affected my decisions for *years*. What might seem like a small realization to some was a massive revelation to me. This corrective experience caused a ripple effect that has allowed me to unlock new levels of self-awareness. Since then, I've reclaimed other parts of my authentic self that my trauma had caused me to abandon, and I have also discovered new parts of myself.

But that's not where the benefits ended; this corrective experience also opened my eyes to just how multifaceted and complex the effects of trauma can be. If I had been wrong about something as simple as why I preferred to wear certain colors, I wondered what else I could be wrong about. What other unchallenged beliefs subconsciously affected my decisions? What other trauma responses were disguising themselves as part of who I am?

I started down an incredible path of self-exploration that emphasized challenging beliefs I had long been adamant about. Of course, I sometimes discovered what I believed about myself was already accurate. But I also learned many new truths about who I am, including activities I enjoy, the type of people I'm willing to let be close to me, my spirituality and views on religion, and so much more. Each new realization makes me feel more whole than the last. I have never felt more secure in who I am, and this security is founded on a non-limiting process. There is nothing I'm unwilling to consider I might be wrong about. All I confidently know about myself thus far is well-founded because it's a result of genuine consideration and self-exploration.

My journey of self-discovery is far from over, but what I've learned so far makes me excited to learn more, free of trauma responses and anything else blocking my connection with my authentic self. I can confidently say I'm continuously figuring out who I am independent of anyone else's expectations or negative influence. I am open-minded, curious, spiritually in tune, and steadfast in learning all I can about myself during my lifetime. I also understand self-discovery is a life-long journey that provides endless opportunities to evolve into newer, better versions of myself if I'm willing to take advantage of this gift.

We have all been influenced by our experiences and interactions with others. Some of your experiences may have caused a disconnect between who you currently are and who you are meant to become. I have learned that genuinely knowing yourself requires looking inside and constructively questioning what you find. Being stubborn and rigid hinders your growth and your healing. Be open to the possibility of being wrong and be willing to let go. This is how you identify behaviors and thought patterns you unknowingly adopted based on other people's beliefs or negativity.

If you want to grow as much as possible during your lifetime, you must be willing to abandon beliefs that do not serve your highest self and cling to and nurture beliefs that do. Thus far, this pursuit has been endlessly rewarding and has given me an even richer life than I could have imagined. It's unbelievable that this journey began simply because my therapist asked, "What don't you like about wearing bright colors?"

The Curse of Trauma

Each of us started life as a unique person, fully dedicated to self-exploration. From birth, our authentic selves lay within us, and the gift of life was our opportunity to discover who we *already* are. If you're ever around young children, you'll quickly notice the pure joy they experience from learning anything new, especially when it's something unique about themselves. This is because self-discovery is central to our life's purpose. This innate drive we all started life with gave us an incredible opportunity to continue tapping into who we were meant to become. However, this drive also made us very susceptible to the influence of others because, as children, we had no frame of reference. We believed whatever we were told to believe about ourselves and others. We were curious but also naïve, which made us vulnerable to misguidance during our journey of self-discovery.

When parents support and nurture their child's individuality and sincerely encourage *internal* exploration, their child can make substantial progress in getting acquainted with their authentic self. The child is also instilled with an enduring sense of identity and self-curiosity that will serve them well throughout adulthood as they connect more deeply with who they are. However, when parents have expectations or beliefs about who they *want* their child to be, specifically regarding their individuality, this promotes a detachment from genuine self-discovery, which will follow the child into adulthood unless unlearned. This is why self-exploration as an adult is imperative.

The earlier trauma occurs, the easier it is to mistake its effects as part of who we are. Our experiences shape our development, so trauma responses that develop early can seem "normal." We assume these responses represent our authentic selves even though they don't. They represent traumatized parts of us. There is usually some part deep inside us that feels like we are not entirely in touch with who we are, but we may struggle to figure out the exact cause on our own.

Trauma responses are behaviors or thought patterns we develop to survive and navigate emotional and psychological distress. They vary from person to person, but here are a few examples of what trauma responses can look like:

- People-pleasing after growing up in an environment where love was highly conditional, and your needs were frequently secondary to other people's needs
- Using alcohol or drugs to dissociate from the ongoing trauma happening in an abusive relationship
- Avoiding social situations (and even developing social anxiety disorder) after being bullied
- Assuming the worst about new people after being hurt in the past, even with little evidence to justify doing so
- Becoming defensive and/or aggressive in response to constructive criticism after growing up with highly defensive parents who rarely took accountability for their actions
- Feeling indifferent about or avoiding relationships after being mistreated or abused
- Being passive after growing up in a home where you were often silenced

It's clear how all these behaviors and thought patterns develop in response to trauma as an attempt to help us "survive." However, it is also clear why continuing them would be psychologically harmful. One thing is true for us all: if we've gone through trauma, we've developed responses to what we went through. As trauma-informed self-love coach Danielle Bernock eloquently stated in *Emerging with Wings*: "Trauma is personal. It does not disappear if it is not validated. When it is ignored or invalidated, the silent screams con-

> **Please note:** Therapy with the *right* therapist for you is *one* of the best ways to discover your trauma responses. We often have blinders and biases regarding ourselves, so engaging in self-analysis with a trusted professional can be helpful.

tinue internally, heard only by the one held captive. When someone enters the pain and hears the screams, healing can begin." [24] In other words, ignoring the effects of your trauma doesn't magically make it go away. The effects will continue to dictate your life until you deliberately work to heal and allow the *right* people to support you on that journey.

When we deny that something affected us, we allow our trauma to influence our thoughts, emotional responses, and behaviors without our full awareness. The worst part is that this often leads to more suffering because our lack of self-awareness prevents us from seeing the connection between our current choices and our trauma. One common way this occurs is with dating patterns. We think, "How did I get here again? I was sure this relationship would be different!"

Until we heal, we will *subconsciously* choose someone compatible with our unhealed trauma responses instead of choosing a partner who is compatible with our healing, authentic selves. This has happened to me, hundreds of my clients, and at least once to most adults. So many of us repeatedly find ourselves in the same kinds of relationships, and we continue to make the same mistakes in our relationships. In hindsight, we may even see how that ex-partner is scarily similar to people who traumatized us in the past, but then we fail to take the next step of questioning what it is that we need to unlearn and heal in order to break this pattern. This happens mainly because our *unhealed* trauma responses will make us "compatible" with people who are like the people who caused the trauma responses to develop in the first place! Our brains are attracted to the familiar, and we are most susceptible when we aren't self-aware. We repeat the same relationship patterns even when we strongly desire something different because the source of these patterns lies within our unresolved trauma.

If we want to find people who are compatible with our healing self, we must do the work to begin healing so that our attraction, thoughts, and behaviors will change. It is very common for a person's "type" to change as they begin healing because they are becoming a different person (for the better.) What they used to find attractive becomes a major turn-off because their unresolved trauma was the thing causing them to find those qualities attractive in the first place. It's like having the veil removed from your eyes, allowing you to finally see clearly about the types of people you have been choosing. This is what happened to me on my healing journey. I used to seek out "bad boys." However, healing helped me see that this title *often* came with toxic masculinity, low emotional intelligence, a lack of integrity, low self-awareness, and poor communication skills. The *complete opposite* of what I truly needed and desired, but I had been conditioned through trauma to believe that this was the type of guy to date. Thankfully, I got help and began healing, so I was able to choose a man who has all the qualities my healing self wants and needs. Thinking back, I now know that I never truly experienced being in love until meeting and choosing my husband, but it makes sense because I was never actually compatible with the other guys; *my trauma was.*

When we don't do self-work first, we create the same outcomes because nothing has changed. It's like using the same blueprint to guide our decisions and expecting a different result than the last time. We will keep dealing with the same issues until we work on improving our relationship with ourselves because the same level of self-understanding and awareness can only lead to the same results. We must work to intimately understand our mentality to improve our choices, thoughts, emotional responses, and behaviors.

With the example of dating, if you want a different experience, you must think critically and uncover what attracts you to the same type of person. You also must figure out what you need to unlearn, heal, and learn for better outcomes.

In this case, you can ask yourself questions like these to develop more self-awareness:

- Am I repeating this pattern because I had emotionally unavailable parents, and that became my standard for what love looks like?
- Did I have experiences that negatively impacted my attachment style?
- Do I fear commitment because my parents divorced?
- Am I subconsciously self-sabotaging my relationships early on so I'm less likely to be disappointed?
- Did I grow up in an environment where I was shamed for being my authentic self, leading me to choose partners with whom I'm not truly compatible?
- Does what I desire my partner to be like actually match what I *need* my partner to be like based on who I currently am and the type of relationship I need to grow as a person?

There are no shortcuts to healing, and good intentions are not enough to avoid the powerful effects of trauma. You must learn to date yourself first, deeply analyze yourself, and correct thoughts and behaviors that contribute to unwanted patterns. It can be tough to come to terms with the effects of your trauma, mainly because doing so can feel retraumatizing. This, among other reasons, is why I strongly encourage you to do your trauma work with a trained professional who can provide the proper support and insight. It is difficult to accept the adverse effects other people caused you (all because they didn't work through their own trauma). It's even more challenging when those people are your parents, siblings, pastor, or other people close to you. Although it's difficult, you reclaim your power by taking accountability for your healing.

You must be willing to relive painful experiences to understand how they shaped you so you can unlearn what you need to unlearn. You heal from trauma by facing the hard truths, processing what occurred in the rawest way to discover its impact on you, abandoning certain beliefs that are rooted in the trauma, and acknowledging your true feelings. Doing so means the difference between living a life of self-awareness and growth or, instead, a life where your unresolved trauma is in charge.

As you learned in Chapter 2, what you ignore and minimize gets to control you subconsciously. And what subconsciously controls you gets to affect your life without your full awareness. One thing I know for sure is regardless of what you've been through, you deserve to reclaim your life. Your trauma has already taken enough from you. Don't allow it to take more.

Healing Your Relationship with Making Mistakes

When you want to learn something new, you must also be willing to make mistakes if you want to figure it out. "Mistake" is just another word for learning opportunity. Mistakes aren't necessarily bad, but depending on how we respond to them, they can lead to bad things for us. They are meant to be part of the learning process. This has been true for you since your birth and will continue to be true for the rest of your life. So, when not embraced and utilized properly, we are at a higher risk of finding ourselves stuck in the same cycle. When we can admit to a mistake and do so gracefully, we can use that experience to help improve our decision-making skills and behaviors going forward. We also find peace with the fact that they are an inevitable part of our lives, which helps us properly regulate our emotions when we make a mistake.

Somewhere along the way, however, many of us developed an aversion to making mistakes, likely because of how adults responded to us making them. For some, this aversion is so strong that they often resist taking accountability for their actions, stunting their personal development. For others, this aversion causes them to avoid new opportunities and experiences, *again* stunting their personal development. Also, for many, this aversion causes them to apologize profusely for everything they do, even when they didn't make a mistake or do anything wrong. Almost as if they view their existence and needs as reasons to remain in an emotional state of constant regret.

This has gotten in the way of our ability to reach our full potential because making mistakes was never supposed to cause us *so much* negative emotion. Sure, as a child, we would sometimes *naturally* feel bad about certain mistakes we made, but those emotions weren't so intense that they stopped us from trying to learn and grow altogether. It wasn't until adults around us responded poorly and sometimes even in severe ways that this led to overwhelming shame and avoidance behavior.

If a parent screams at their child for accidentally breaking something or spilling their drink, *frequent* responses like this gradually alter how the child emotionally responds to their own mistakes. Of course, we want to learn to feel and express empathy if our mistakes emotionally affect someone else (and parents have a profound responsibility to teach and model perspective-taking and empathy), but being *conditioned* to feel *deep* shame, especially from developmentally impossible expectations, can cause a child to grow into an adult that views even the simplest mistake or embarrassment as justification for the harshest of self-punishment.

Sure, because we are all unique, complex individuals, some children may *naturally* be more prone to feeling shame from simple mistakes, even if their parents have an appropriate response. However, parents still have a responsibility to help their children develop a healthy balance between holding themselves accountable for their actions, having good discernment to assess the gravity of their actions, having empathy for others impacted by their actions, and having compassion for themselves as they learn from their mistakes. It's a delicate balance, but the responsibility falls on those raising the child to teach them cognitive flexibility in this way and to nurture their emotional intelligence so they can have a healthy relationship with making mistakes.

Unsurprisingly, helping a child achieve this delicate balance largely depends on how the parent verbally and behaviorally responds to them, as well as how they help the child understand other people's poor responses. Their parent's response *is* the lesson. It sets the foundation for the child's own responses in the future, not only toward themselves but even toward others. Kids learn from what we say to them and what we do to them, so if we model that they should feel *great* shame and guilt for every mistake they make, this will become their internal compass on how to navigate mistakes as adults. How can we expect them to have a different emotional response if ours was teaching them that their mistakes merited what we modeled?

How did the adults in your life respond to your childhood mistakes? Did they yell at you? Did they call you names or say you were a bad kid? Did they hit you? Those types of reactions can create a severe negative emotional relationship with making mistakes, known as toxic shame (experiencing shame in response to events that should not call for such a strong emotional reaction).

Like all your emotions, shame communicates important things to you, but traumatic experiences can negatively alter that communication.

Shame, like all your emotions, influences your behavior and is based on your thoughts. You are supposed to feel sincere regret and even guilt when you do something you *consciously know* is wrong. You should also always hold yourself accountable for your actions and choices. But again, shame is a very intense emotion that has the risk of negatively impacting self-esteem, especially when experienced in response to an action that does not *actually* call for such a high level of emotional distress. It is not something we are meant to feel frequently (unless we are *truly* doing things that rationally merit that emotion).

Under healthy circumstances, shame is reserved for the most horrible of offenses. Plus, this only applies when a person is actually old enough to understand and consistently manage their actions. Due to brain development, early childhood is not one of these times, and even middle childhood through adolescence won't be, in some cases, depending on the specific circumstances. In other words, it is crucial to have developmentally sensitive expectations of minor-aged humans and for teaching to be a central part of implementing natural consequences as part of learning self-accountability (such as having your toddler clean up a wall they drew on, then acknowledging their desire to draw, explaining why it is not okay to draw on the wall, and then showing them appropriate ways to meet their drawing needs in the future).

By making teaching the main priority, over time, a child also begins to engage in significantly less undesirable behaviors (many of which will stop altogether, such as drawing on the wall) because they develop an internal understanding without developing harmful emotional responses like toxic shame; this is how we teach accountability without causing harm in the process. Our brains should not be *conditioned* to produce shame in response to typical day-to-day mistakes, as this is not the purpose of that emotion. However, as we have discussed, our experiences can alter how our brains respond over time to events in our lives, including being conditioned to have a more intense emotional response to making a mistake.

Let's review the actual definitions of these three emotions:

- **Regret:** feel sad, repentant, or disappointed (over something that has happened or been done, especially a loss or missed opportunity).
- **Guilt:** a feeling of having done wrong or failed in an obligation.
- **Shame:** a painful feeling of humiliation or distress caused by the consciousness of wrong or foolish behavior.

In most cases, regret and guilt are appropriate and proportionate emotional responses to making a mistake, as this is not the same as intentional wrongdoing. All three of these emotions are meant to help you use the experience as a learning opportunity of some kind. However, shame is particularly intense because it is meant to keep you mindful of choosing behaviors that align with good character. We all do things that go against our character and values, so *healthy* levels of shame exist to help us have a way to better monitor ourselves for behaviors that don't fit who we are or, better yet, who we are trying to become.

The problem is that what is considered "good character" can vary greatly depending on who is defining it, and someone's behaviors toward you after a mistake sends you non-verbal messages about their definition. Overall, I think most humans agree that qualities like empathy, integrity, kindness, respect, etc., are all signs of good character. However, as children, we had to be taught these things and, better yet, needed to be given adequate time to learn these lessons based on what was developmentally possible for our current age. For instance, the average human cannot *consistently* regulate "big" emotions until around five or six years old, and that is only in cases where this skill is being nurtured over time in a healthy, effective way by the parents. So, suppose a child is being raised (and reprimanded instead of being taught) by a parent who has developmentally unrealistic expectations or, worse, abusive reactions. In that case, the risk of conditioning toxic shame is high.

Early childhood is a very vulnerable time during which toxic shame and guilt can develop. When young children feel great shame from a parent's responses to the child simply trying to learn about the world, this causes healthy shame and guilt to grow into toxic shame and guilt. Young children do not yet have the mental capacity to *consistently know* right from wrong, and they understand very little about the world as a whole. Before age six, due to the stages of brain development and the amount of time it takes to learn, kids are largely pre-operational in their thinking, which means they are less likely to think out plans and imagine the consequences of their decisions. This is why your four-year-old might insist on going outside without a jacket in the middle of winter. (Literally, *everything* has to be taught repeatedly over time in order for a human to develop the skill of doing it well independently, so yes, we even have to be trained how to think – this is also why so many adults struggle with critical thinking because they were never properly taught during their upbringing and still haven't taken the time to learn. Because of ineffective parenting and even abuse, despite biological aging, some adults' mental and emotional ages are still that of a child. They are still pre-operational in their thinking, which leads to poor outcomes in their lives, and the shame around admitting when they are wrong keeps them from doing the work to mentally mature.)

Many of us were severely punished for actions we developmentally couldn't fully understand yet, even if we wanted to. That would be like me punishing my toddler son for not knowing calculus. Some children receive these responses from their parents starting as young as two years old, so it's easy to see how this would be the "perfect" recipe for toxic shame and guilt.

Sincerely try to think back to your level of understanding when you were still in the single digits. Between zero and ten years old, there was so much you didn't understand and behaviors you engaged in without much reasoning or thought. As a young kid, your brain took significantly longer to process information, so making frequent mistakes was an inevitable part of development during that stage of life. Your brain was nowhere near fully developed; this doesn't happen until the mid-to-late twenties. You didn't yet *fully* understand cause and effect or right and wrong, which are the result of being *consistently taught* emotional intelligence as the brain develops over the *years*. You also hadn't yet developed impulse control. Since this involves emotional regulation, it doesn't become more of a *consistent* skill until around six or seven years old. Again, that's only the case in homes where parents *teach* their children with a healthy, effective approach that does not involve violence or abuse. These skills also take well into adulthood to mature.

An unhealthy relationship with shame can follow a person for a lifetime if they never do the self-work to heal. This unhealthy complex can cause the child to grow into a people pleaser, constantly overextending themselves and changing their behavior to meet the demands or needs of others at the cost of their own well-being. It can condition the child's nervous system to create more anxiety around other people out of fear of being judged or making a mistake, which can turn into a social anxiety disorder. It can cause them to quickly become defensive when someone holds them accountable for things they've done wrong. Being called out, even thoughtfully, can make them feel attacked because they've developed such a negative association with making mistakes due to how their parents responded to them growing up.

In these cases, the parent's go-to response was usually one of two extremes, the first of which is the whole "my baby can do no wrong" approach to parenting, which *conditions* a child to rarely feel responsible for their actions (so they consequently rarely feel guilt, shame, or regret). In other words, the parent (or parents) was permissive, letting the child do whatever without taking the time to create structure and teach them alternative ways to express their emotions and meet their goals. They rarely, if ever, held their kid accountable for their actions in a healthy way.

A permissive parent is told their kid hit someone at school, and they get defensive instead of holding the child accountable in an empathetic but direct way. They also fail to teach and model healthy ways to express anger. Since the parent doesn't help their child truly digest the impact of their actions, the child then fails to experience accountability and a healthy emotional response, like guilt or regret. A permissive parent often fails to model healthy behaviors and lets their kid do whatever they want without teaching them how to problem-solve, think through their choices, and empathize with others. This can lead to the child growing into an entitled, selfish adult who has little care for others, projects their accountability onto others, and rarely feels healthy amounts of shame, even when it's merited based on their actions. If the trauma is impactful enough, it can even lead to the development of narcissistic personality disorder or other mental health conditions that are a product of trauma and poor parenting.

The other extreme parenting style is the "because I said so" approach to parenting, which has the opposite effect and *conditions* intense experiences of shame, regret, and guilt that are not appropriate. This includes being authoritarian and punishing the child, sometimes with spanking or other physical violence, for developmentally expected behaviors instead of truly disciplining and teaching them alternative ways to express feelings and meet goals.

The authoritarian parent has little patience or empathy for their child and is ill-informed about what is developmentally expected or possible for the child, based on the child's age and brain development thus far. They frequently label developmentally normal behaviors that *all kids* of that age do as a "sign" that their child is a "bad kid" and that they need to beat them so they can become a "good kid." They don't teach the child through in-depth explanation, natural consequences, or modeling the appropriate behaviors.

They mistakenly believe that they are "teaching" because their child may stop the unwanted actions, but this is not due to them actually learning anything. Instead, the child is in a state of fear, which puts them in survival mode and causes them to develop trauma responses. Just like any human who is being hit would do, they stop the behaviors to avoid more abuse. As a result, the parent has a false sense of successfully teaching despite not actually teaching anything. But in reality, their child fails to *thoroughly* learn essential skills within a developmentally expected timeline, including critical thinking, empathy, problem-solving, emotional regulation, healthy emotional expression, and emotional intelligence. The child is also left with adverse psychological and emotional effects. Humans learn the same way we do in school, by being taught through repetition, explanation, patience, processing, modeling, and natural consequences (to understand cause and effect.)

The way the trauma response manifests depends on several factors, including how the child, with their limited understanding, attempts to interpret what's happening and why, as well as the frequency of the parent's harmful responses. Regardless of how the trauma response manifests in an individual, the initial cause is still an aversion to being wrong or making mistakes that grew out of a parent's poor reactions to mistakes during the person's upbringing (either from the parent not encouraging accountability or from the parent demonizing the child for typical mistakes and failing to use those moments as learning opportunities.) A child develops these trauma responses to try to navigate these experiences with their parent since, developmentally, the child is unable to meet their parent's expectation of not making mistakes (either the child rarely acknowledges the mistakes they make because their parents don't or the child feels toxic shame anytime they do make a mistake because of how their parents react).

Once the child grows up, that negative association with making mistakes has been solidified. Without trauma work and heightened self-awareness, they will continue to live life trying to avoid discomfort from making a mistake or being wrong, not realizing this aversion holds them back from growth and positive self-development. The adults in their lives should have helped them healthily move through emotions like shame and guilt, not minimize or amplify them by responding to mistakes in such harmful ways.

The saddest part is that a parent's tendency to do this to their child usually originates from adults who did the same to them as a child, creating a cycle of generational trauma until someone learns and does better. You have to normalize the learning process by accepting that your mistakes are opportunities for learning and growth. Doing so is critical because when you avoid the discomfort of being wrong, you tend to make more mistakes that you also fail to learn or grow from. It can become a lifetime cycle of struggling with the same issues within yourself and your relationships.

Mistakes are an inevitable part of life, so humans suffer when they fall into either extreme of the spectrum (being utterly defensive when making a mistake or being overly avoidant of ever making one). We have to be in the middle so we can be intentional about remaining mindful of our actions while also understanding the value of learning from our attempts. We have to unlearn this toxic conditioning and reparent ourselves into a better mental space by responding to ourselves the way our parents (and whoever else) failed to.

If you weren't taught the delicate balance during your upbringing, as an adult, you now have the responsibility to begin teaching it to yourself. Just as if you had been taught as a child, learning this will take time, patience, consistency, explanation, and correction. You do this by being mindful of how you respond verbally (self-talk) and behaviorally when you make mistakes. You refrain from making excuses because that encourages a defensive mindset, and you refrain from demonizing yourself because that encourages a shame mindset.

Additionally, when it comes to avoiding a defensive mindset, you also have to be mindful not to twist other people's words to deflect from taking accountability for your actions. People often will do this in response to others trying to hold them accountable for things they actually did, but when we do this, we fail to grow and also damage our relationships. If someone genuinely brings something to your attention that you truly are accountable for (meaning you are not being gaslit), take a breath, have humility, and listen to what they share about their experience of you. We have to be willing to take constructive feedback from others who are well-intentioned and capable of giving a rational view. There is so much we can learn about our growth areas from hearing someone else's experience of us.

In order to pull yourself to the middle of the emotional spectrum, when something occurs that you are genuinely accountable for (meaning *your* actions or words), you have to take accountability and be honest with yourself about your intentions. Then, you must *privately* (to yourself) honor those intentions to protect your self-esteem but also understand that they are *secondary* to any significant pain your mistake may have caused. Then, *sincerely* apologize to any affected parties, fully owning what you did or said, and *do not* use your intentions as a way to deflect from responsibility. You don't get to decide whether you hurt someone because it is their experience. Lastly, you must reflect on your mistakes to uncover the valuable lessons they hold and commit to applying those lessons in the future so you avoid preventable patterns of behavior. If the specific mistake was truly preventable, continuing to do it repeatedly no longer counts as a mistake. Once we have learned better, we have to hold ourselves accountable to doing better (*but* also remember that, depending on the circumstances, someone can be hurt or disappointed by a decision you made, such as canceling plans, and it doesn't *always* mean you did something wrong – you should still validate and hold space for their feelings, but you aren't at fault).

You also have to have discernment and realize that sometimes a mistake won't hold any valuable lesson other than it being a gentle reminder of your humanity. If you accidentally break something, it is because you are human and not because you are a terrible person. The lesson is that you have to give yourself grace and remember that no matter how careful you are, you will still make *innocent* mistakes throughout your life. Making mistakes helps you learn, and you have to see their value; otherwise, you'll limit your growth. You are meant to use them as a source of self-development, so don't let them go to waste. Use them as intended and allow them to help you continuously evolve as a person.

Taking Accountability

Our trauma responses are not always as innocent as a change in color preference. Certain traumatic experiences cause us to develop responses that, when unchecked, cause other people trauma. For instance, being in an abusive relationship can lead the abused person to engage in similar behaviors. Think about it; if someone suffers verbal abuse, they may begin to do the same to protect themselves.

Suppose someone grows up witnessing the people around them engaging in abusive behavior. This can subconsciously normalize this behavior, making that person more susceptible to doing the same (or ending up in a relationship where they're similarly abused). This is because our closest relationships are our growth environments. Who we choose to surround ourselves with can have a major impact on how much and in what ways we grow or not. Just like a flower, we can only bloom under the right conditions. Staying in certain relationships or environments will cause us to wither until we change environments and heal. Psychological research has confirmed this many times over.

A research article from the National Institute of Justice, "Children Exposed to Violence," states: "Exposure to violence can harm a child's emotional, psychological, and even physical development. Children exposed to violence are more likely to have difficulty in school, abuse drugs or alcohol, act aggressively, suffer from depression or other mental health problems, and engage in criminal behavior as adults." [25]

The adverse effects and outcomes of abuse and violence are well-known and have been repeatedly validated through research. If you've experienced this or any related trauma, you will need to do some self-work. You can't have healthy relationships without first working to heal trauma responses that would harm your relationships. I learned this lesson the hard way. Before meeting my husband, I was in an abusive romantic relationship for three years. Without realizing it, I picked up some emotionally and psychologically abusive behaviors from spending those years with that person. These were harmful trauma responses that would have affected my relationships going forward if they weren't unlearned.

When I first began dating my husband, these toxic communication patterns showed up in our relationship. When we first met, my brain was still responding to the relationship environment I had come from, and I had to learn how to respond to my new relationship. I had to consciously help my brain accept that I no longer needed those trauma responses because I was no longer in an abusive relationship. I learned by being aware of my choices, processing and analyzing my trauma to understand how the previous relationship affected me, and consistently correcting my behaviors and thoughts so I could break the patterns.

Thankfully, my husband was patient and understanding, and I was intentional about unlearning and healing. I chose to take accountability, and with practice, I improved my communication significantly and abandoned those harmful behaviors. I also believed in my ability to change, which was especially important. Otherwise, I would have been at risk of a self-fulfilling prophecy (more on this in the next chapter). Now, my husband and I have a very healthy communication style because of the intentional work I did to correct and heal at the beginning of our relationship.

I stated in the introduction that we are not responsible for our trauma, but we are responsible for our healing. Part of taking responsibility is looking with humility and honesty at thoughts and behaviors we need to change. It's tempting to be defensive about it, but if we choose that approach, our relationships and overall quality of life will suffer as a consequence.

A significant part of healing is taking accountability for our behaviors, even the ones we aren't proud of. Our behaviors are choices, which means they are in our control. When we make excuses for not changing harmful behaviors, we create a mental barrier that prevents change. Change requires no longer self-defining by our past behaviors. When we continue to self-define that way, we accidentally condition ourselves to continue the behavior. Behavioral change takes a lot of hard work and mental preparation, so how we talk to ourselves is imperative.

Take these two statements, for example:

Person #1: "I've always had a bad attitude. I was raised not to take no b.s. from anyone. If someone tries me, I won't hesitate to curse them out."

Person #2: "I give respect, so I don't tolerate disrespect. I'm working on communicating my anger in an effective, healthy way. I still have a way to go, but I'm taking every opportunity to grow, practice this skill, and improve."

Which of these two people sounds like they will make progress toward change? Of course, the answer is person #2! You can't expect to change if you refuse to take self-accountability or commit to change. Remember: you are always listening to yourself. Speaking like person #1 primes you to justify and continue the behavior. In contrast, talking to yourself like person #2 keeps you self-aware and accountable. The change will take time and happen gradually, but you will only progress by taking ownership of your desire for change.

Of course, you will still be tempted to engage in the old behavior because you have become accustomed to it. However, you're more likely to catch yourself when you maintain a high level of self-awareness, like person #2. The more you talk to yourself and self-reflect, the more self-aware you become. If you're dismissive about changing, you will become less self-aware because you aren't invested, and as a result, you won't change.

Mental preparation and commitment are the foundation for change. You cannot change overnight, but you can start progressing by tomorrow. Change comes with noticeable progress that is relatively consistent despite old habits occasionally occurring. Over time, these old habits should lessen as you continue to master new skills through practice.

Practice how you want to be so you can become who you desire to become. Self-growth results from choosing to shift your mindset, practicing new ways of responding to your emotions, and engaging in new behaviors. Whatever you want to improve about yourself is simply a *skill*. No different than if you wanted to learn how to play piano or how to bake. Before you know it, that skill will become an embodied trait that is now part of who you are. We develop new skills and make positive progress by committing to change, having patience with ourselves, learning from each attempt (or mistake), and holding ourselves accountable to consistently practicing.

The first step to lasting change is to stop self-identifying with the trait you want to improve because your self-talk significantly impacts your beliefs and behaviors. In other words, the more you tell yourself something about yourself, the more it becomes an identity instead of a growth area (something you want to improve). For example, if you frequently make statements like "I am an anxious person" or "I am always quick to anger," you will unintentionally encourage yourself to stay that way. Your thoughts are indeed that powerful! How you speak to yourself is like giving your brain an order, so when you command it to stay the same (by continuously self-defining by traits you want to improve), making progress becomes challenging.

Of course, you should always acknowledge your growth areas, but thankfully, you can do this without creating a self-limiting mindset. Self-defining by your current skill level only stops you from improving because you convince yourself there's no more room for improvement. So, instead of saying, "I am an anxious person," which would be self-identifying by something you want to improve, say, "I sometimes struggle with anxiety, and I'm working on managing it better." The second statement acknowledges that you are more than just your anxiety (because you are!), and anxiety is an emotion that, with practice, can be well-managed (because it can!).

You can even take it a step further and say, "I am figuring out what triggers my anxiety so I can find ways to improve how I manage those feelings in the moment." By choosing better words to describe your experiences, you can shift how you see and respond to those experiences. Use words as a tool to prime yourself for change, not defeat. Change is already challenging enough, so you don't want to accidentally create more barriers for yourself through your chosen language. The goal of self-talk is to leave the door open for change and increase your feelings of self-efficacy.

Defining who you are only by your struggles subconsciously leads to a defeated mindset. It makes it seem like this is the only way you can be, but that is not the case. Your growth areas are not your identity; they are opportunities for self-improvement. Emotional regulation, for instance, is a skill, so you can better manage your emotions with practice. When it comes to anxiety, practicing thought replacement, doing gradual exposure exercises for corrective experiences, consciously accepting that you're capable of growth and change, meditating, practicing affirmations, seeking knowledge to increase emotional intelligence, and engaging in other healing work can *all* help a person improve their anxiety management. After all, I would know because

I used to have a pretty severe anxiety disorder myself, and I practiced skills like these to overcome it. I am now significantly better at managing anxiety when it does occur because my skill set has improved.

There is so much more to you than the thoughts and behaviors you're battling. No matter what they may be, they are not all of who you are. They're simply parts of you that you would like to, and can, improve. After all, our goal isn't to become less human because that's impossible. Our goal is to gain a deeper understanding of our humanity and become a better manager of ourselves by improving our skills through practice. Practice makes progress (because perfection is a myth and goes against what it means to be human). We are perfectly imperfect, and it's all about learning how to accept and work well with those imperfections. When we better understand the workings of our mind and practice these skills, we begin to have better responses when moments of mental difficulty arise.

The second step to creating lasting change is to ensure your expectations are realistic and practice self-compassion. Change happens gradually, not perfectly, and mistakes are a normal part of the process. Difficult moments should be seen as learning opportunities so you can apply what you learned when the next opportunity comes. This happens by self-reflecting on what occurred and why it occurred. What were you feeling and thinking at the time? What triggered that particular response? What could you do differently in the future that would meet your needs and also align with your growth goals? In hindsight, is there something you can do now that would align with who you are becoming, such as putting your pride aside, taking accountability, and sincerely apologizing?

Think back to when you were a child learning to walk for the first time. (I want to acknowledge this example does not apply to everyone, so please replace walking with a different skill you mastered early in life if needed.) If you hadn't accepted falling as part of the learning process, you wouldn't have learned to walk, or at least not as quickly as you did. And it wouldn't have been because you weren't capable of learning but simply because you *believed* you couldn't just because you fell. Having such a belief would have been enough to stop you from trying to improve your skills.

You know how to walk today because, as a child, you didn't see falling as the be-all and end-all. You probably fell over one hundred times, but you used each fall as an opportunity to learn how to stand and walk better. You acknowledged your progress, no matter how small it may have seemed to you or others. As you repeatedly tried to walk, you altered your technique until you eventually learned how to do it. Because of this, today, you can confidently say, "I know how to walk well," even though that's not how you began. You only know how to walk now because you never allowed falling to create a self-limiting belief. And to this day, even if you happened to trip and fall, it wouldn't change your opinion that you know how to walk.

Too often, we allow unrealistic expectations to cause us to discount our progress. Our growth maximizes when we celebrate all our milestones and gracefully hold ourselves accountable. Being responsible for our change does not mean we shouldn't be self-compassionate. Giving ourselves grace is essential because mistakes are an inevitable part of learning, and if we don't accept this, we create unrealistic expectations that unintentionally hinder our growth.

If you often find it easier to give grace to others than to give it to yourself, an excellent way to practice this skill is to talk to yourself in the third person and by name. Using third person, ask yourself what you would say to someone else in the same situation to encourage them and help them see what they've already accomplished, no matter how "small."

For instance, if you struggle with anger but you find it's getting easier to apologize, celebrate that. That is change; that is growth! Celebrating your success helps you build momentum for more change because it enables you to see yourself and your capabilities differently.

Say to yourself, "I am so proud of (your name) for apologizing and owning up to their mistakes! They made the right decision, and I know they can keep it up. That moment proved they can do more if they keep working on it."

Most importantly, after you say it, allow the words to sit with you. Reflect on them and accept that you're talking to *yourself*. As a mantra, tell yourself, "Those words are for me, and that is how I feel about myself." Doing so helps you internalize the words even though you said them in the third person.

The third-person approach allows you to practice getting comfortable speaking to yourself differently by using a skill you already have (giving others grace) and applying it to yourself in a way that may feel less uncomfortable. Third-person language mimics what it's like to speak to someone else even though you're talking to yourself. It's like tricking your brain by using one skill to build on another. Over time, as you get more comfortable, you can graduate to second-person language (using "you" statements) and then first-person (using "I" statements).

It might feel silly, but when you're trying to learn, you have to meet yourself where you are and be open to unconventional ways of meeting your goals. Flexibility and creativity can help you find ways to meet your needs while you grow. For example, when I had an anxiety disorder, I practiced getting comfortable with difficult conversations by sitting side by side (no eye contact) with my husband. (Keep in mind that "comfortable" doesn't mean I now like difficult conversations. It means I'm fully willing to have them and skilled at the process because I've practiced).

In my practice, my goal was to say the most challenging part. I focused on those one or two words because I knew saying them would allow my anxiety to ease a bit, making it easier for me to elaborate. Although still anxiety-provoking, it felt more doable to break the conversation down to the small task of just getting the hard part out. Also, doing so resulted in reassurance and validation from my husband, which helped my anxiety ease even more.

At the time, my anxiety disorder made me feel like having uncomfortable conversations would be the worst thing ever. Getting the words out provided me with the corrective experience I needed to proceed because I realized it wasn't as bad as my anxiety made it feel. I would tell myself, "I just have to say two words! The rest will be much easier. I am allowed to take my time, but I have to say it." This is what the combination of giving yourself grace while holding yourself accountable looks like.

Because of how my anxiety was then, I needed time and no eye contact to get tough statements out. I didn't judge myself for it. I accepted where I was on my growth journey and acknowledged that if I wanted to be somewhere else, I had to find a creative, doable way to push myself. I also made sure to internalize the experience afterward. I had conversations with myself and with my husband to reflect on what actually happened as compared to the lies I had told myself in response to feeling anxious. Internalizing my corrective experiences helped me feel more confident each time, and I made progress as a result.

I took my time and gave myself grace. Initially, it sometimes took twenty minutes of breathing, crying, reassuring myself, my husband reassuring me, and sitting silently together, but I always got it out! And quickly, over time, that twenty minutes became fifteen, then five, and now we easily have face-to-face conversations about any and everything. I also now feel confident having difficult conversations with others too! (Even though it's still not my favorite thing to do and never will be). All because I allowed myself to practice a skill while meeting my current needs, celebrated each victory, lovingly pushed myself out of my comfort zone, regularly challenged myself, and through processing, internalized the corrective experiences I had each time.

The third and final step to creating lasting change is to engage in regular self-reflection. Change requires processing because processing is how we remember (internalize) what we learned. You want to process *repeatedly* so it truly sticks with you. It's just like studying for a test. The more you review the information, in this case, what you learned about yourself from the situation, the better you will remember what you need to do differently next time. When you fail to process your experiences, you fail to learn vital information about your mental and behavioral habits. And if you don't have that knowledge, how can you progressively work toward change? You can't.

When you consciously practice being who you want to become, you give yourself the best chance at making as much progress as possible. I can't guarantee you'll reach every self-development goal you have within your lifetime. However, I assure you that you can and will meet many, and even for the ones you don't, you can make meaningful progress. Growth is guaranteed if you are willing to practice skills that will help you become more of who you desire to be and abandon self-limiting beliefs that are holding you back from becoming. After all, you are capable and have endless growth potential through the power of your chosen thoughts and behaviors. You just have to decide how many times you want to evolve into a better version of yourself.

It's very simple. If you don't believe you can change, you won't work toward change. If I thought I was a failure, I would begin to feel and act like someone who thinks they're a failure. The good news is that the new belief doesn't have to be strong for you to progress. If the best you can do with where you are is say, "I am willing to accept I could be wrong about my capabilities," you can still make progress! If you're at least willing to consider that how you feel isn't always an indicator of what's possible, that's enough to get started.

I'm sure the first time you did a school performance or went on a date, you had intrusive thoughts that made you feel incapable, but you later realized it wasn't as bad as you thought it would be. You were willing to practice, learn, and adapt, and because of this, you got better. As you push yourself and prove what you are capable of (even when your intrusive thoughts tell you otherwise), your belief in yourself will strengthen on its own! A mustard seed of faith is enough to get you started, and with commitment, it can snowball into a mountain of confidence over time.

What you believe is possible shapes your becoming. You cannot achieve anything new by doing what you already do. You have to identify changes you want to make and then take steps (no matter the size) toward the goal. You also must celebrate every victory along the way (no matter the size) and see mistakes as learning opportunities that will only sharpen your skills.

If perfection is your goal, you will constantly feel like you're failing. However, if learning is your goal, you will continuously feel like you're growing. Apply all you learn, and use the power of your *chosen* thoughts as a stepping stone to better versions of yourself. There is always more you can do. Don't see your growth as a destination. It's a journey that only ends if you decide to stop working on yourself.

Other Key Points to Achieve Lasting Change

Practicing a new way of being doesn't mean "fake it until you make it." I don't want you to fake anything or lie to yourself in any way. I want you to meet yourself where you are and identify small changes you can make to improve. Then, with self-compassion, hold yourself accountable for those changes.

The issue with the "fake it until you make it" approach is that it suggests you can change overnight, and that's not realistic. For instance, expecting yourself to fake having confidence will likely cause you more distress. Instead, make gradual changes to practice building your self-esteem, such as wearing clothes that make you feel good, practicing daily affirmations, spending more time engaging in your talents, or finding a new hobby for an additional sense of purpose. Taking these kinds of actions exposes you to more positive emotions and experiences, which allows your confidence to grow (if you also internalize and change how you talk to yourself).

Growth is about *practicing* until you make it. With any skill, you must understand your goals, learn what you need to do to achieve them (this is where the importance of understanding psychology and the brain comes in), and then take steps toward change. Most of the time, what stops you from changing is the mental barrier of believing it's just who you are or the knowledge barrier of believing you can change but just not knowing how to do it yet. In most cases, psychology removes these barriers by helping you realize you can make changes if you learn how the mind works and by using the tools this knowledge provides.

That old saying "knowledge is power" is true! For example, do you know who is the least susceptible to manipulation? Someone who understands the psychology behind manipulation tactics! If you know gaslighting, triangulation, love bombing, projection, and other psychological terms and, most importantly, how and under what circumstances those behaviors typically manifest, you can better identify when someone uses one of those tactics. Sure, knowing doesn't mean it could never happen or that you couldn't misjudge someone, but it absolutely makes it significantly less likely and provides us with the best protection! It also decreases the likelihood that the person would get away with doing those things for a very long time before you are able to identify and label what they are doing. Before I knew what fire was, I wasn't afraid to touch it. It was only once I learned what it was that I *truly* understood why I shouldn't.

Understanding the information in this book and seeking additional information on psychology, the human brain, and similar topics are essential steps to truly understanding who you are and building the skills to help you navigate life and manage yourself better. **Just because the traumatic event is "over" doesn't mean you are automatically free of its residual effects.** Trauma responses can and often do persist after the traumatic events have stopped, especially when you haven't processed your trauma. They don't just magically disappear; they have to be deliberately unlearned. If you aren't careful, you can begin to see these trauma responses as part of your identity, as I did with not liking bright colors.

A good practice is to remain open to getting to know yourself. Accept that what you know about yourself might change, and that's okay. It's part of the self-development journey, so don't resist it. You don't want to mistakenly convince yourself that you know everything about yourself because you don't. Allow yourself to be curious and accept that your identity is constantly evolving, and your true beliefs likely lie in the gray (not the extremes of black-and-white). Practicing this mindset helps you identify your trauma responses because it keeps you in a state of willingness and exploration.

As I stated earlier, there are too many trauma responses for me to name them all. Plus, trauma responses are specific to each person's experiences and can manifest differently from person to person despite overarching similarities. In other words, they are nuanced. Because of this, you must be willing to push yourself outside your comfort zone and seek new experiences to help with the unlearning process. Unlearning is no easy feat; remember to seek support and continuously seek knowledge (just like you are by reading this book) to help you on your healing journey. **You are capable of change.** I often use this example with my clients. If someone offered you one million dollars to commit to a behavioral change for a month, would you do it? I have yet to have a client say anything other than, "Yeah because I want the money!" If you can change your behavior for money, you can change your behavior, period. Often, the issue is that you lack motivation, not ability.

The motivation is there; you just aren't always mindful of it. Your true motivation for change is a better life and relationship with yourself. You must consistently remind yourself of the value and the benefits you'll gain, personally, socially, and spiritually, from growth. The outcomes of putting in the work to change dramatically exceed one million dollars. It's priceless!

Yes, you will need to do things that make you very uncomfortable. Yes, you will have to let go of relationships that are holding you back and, as a result, go through a period of grief. Yes, you will have to face hard truths, but when you think about what you can gain, it likely will be worth it. After all, we're talking about your life satisfaction, relationships, experiences, and connection with yourself. That's everything that matters. I have yet to have any client regret a hard decision that was also the best decision; often, the only regret is not choosing to do it sooner. Storms truly do lead to rainbows, especially when you purposefully and intentionally choose a storm that will better your life in the long run.

Plus, dedicating yourself to growth and continuing to evolve into your authentic self may lead to you finding your way to become a millionaire on your own one day. Now that would be great!

Regularly ask yourself processing questions. You can reach new heights when you're willing to look inward. As you self-reflect, you begin to recognize your ability to create a satisfying and fulfilling life through your choices. You also seek relationships with people living similarly, and you learn to set boundaries with those not doing the same to prevent them from getting in the way of your growth.

There are only two ways to live life: either with your unresolved trauma in control (subconsciously) or your healing self in control (consciously). It's clear which is the best option. Healing is intentional, so when you choose that route, you can keep bringing what's hidden in your subconscious to the surface. The goal is to empty your subconscious as much as humanly possible so you can have very little affecting your behaviors, thoughts, and emotions without your awareness. You have to understand the impact of your trauma on your psyche to regain control over its effects. Knowing how these experiences have shaped you allows you to restore your power and heal. Questions like these can help you self-reflect and identify parts of yourself that you may need to explore more deeply to get closer to your authentic self:

- When did you first notice certain behaviors or thought patterns emerging?
- Why did you choose your current career path?
- What experiences in your life have either helped or hurt your self-esteem?
- How did you see yourself as a child compared to how you see yourself now?
- Why did your self-image change?
- Is there anything about how you used to see yourself that you need to reclaim?
- Where do your current beliefs come from?
- Have you openly explored and challenged your beliefs, or are they simply a product of your conditioning?

Be curious about why you choose to do what you do. Try to connect the dots between your current choices and past experiences. Some of what you find through self-reflection will be insignificant, but some of it will be crucial information that can help you improve yourself and your life.

CHAPTER 7

Self-Fulfilling Prophecies

*If we believe something enough, we can create
it, but that's not always a good thing.*

By this point, you know your thoughts have a powerful influence over your emotions and behaviors. Because of this influence, things can go wrong if you're not mindful of the thoughts you choose to nurture. One of the ways this happens is through self-fulfilling prophecies. A self-fulfilling prophecy is when you turn your beliefs into reality through your behaviors.

Let's say you believe no one would want to be your friend. In most cases, when someone has an opinion like this, it results from a traumatic experience, like bullying. If you had this belief, emotionally, you would begin to feel negative feelings like sadness and loneliness. And behaviorally, you would likely avoid connecting with others because you would believe it's pointless. But here's the thing. The *main* reason the belief would come true is due to its influence on your choices. If you choose to isolate and disconnect, then no, you won't have friends. It's not that you *can't* have friends, but that you make choices that prevent you from finding and forming friendships. As a result, your belief becomes true; thus, a self-fulfilling prophecy occurs.

To prevent the self-fulfilling prophecy from continuing, you would need to change your mindset. Here is a healthier, more accurate belief: "I have been struggling to make friends, but in recent years, I have to admit I stopped trying. People have made me feel like an outcast in the past, so I've been afraid to connect with others. However, I no longer want to be lonely. I need to find ways to connect with people who share things in common with me. My community is out there. I just haven't found them yet." It is clear how this mindset would lead to a behavioral shift. A person who speaks to themselves this way will seek out new relationships and apply what they have learned from past attempts.

The problem in the past was that you couldn't find people similar to you, but those people do exist. You might use social media or attend events where you can find people who share your interests and have similar personalities. This perspective will eventually lead to more friendships because the mental barrier is lifted, and you're making an effort to seek relationships.

Sure, other things may contribute to a person's struggle to make friends. Perhaps they need to work on some of their behaviors, but, again, if a person is willing, skills can be improved in most cases. Remember: we all have self-work to do, but if we are willing to grow and change, we can improve our lives. The research on self-fulfilling prophecies proves we become what we believe we are. It also helps us understand how changing who we believe we are can alter who we become.

The word "prophecy" means a prediction about the future. There are two kinds of self-fulfilling prophecies: self-imposed and other-imposed. As you can probably determine from the terms, they're distinguished by who imposes the belief that leads to the outcome. The example I just gave is one of a self-imposed self-fulfilling prophecy, a belief about yourself that directly impacts how you act. In contrast, other-imposed self-fulfilling prophecies represent the relationship between how people treat you and the direct impact that has on how you act. It's also important to note that this means you have the same influence on other people. Simply put, the way you treat someone has a direct impact on how that person might respond.

Other-Imposed Self-Fulfilling Prophecies

Your beliefs and behaviors directly influence other people's actions all the time and vice versa. For instance, when you go into a situation expecting someone to behave a certain way, you're more likely to act in a manner that increases the chances of the other person exhibiting that expected behavior. Let's say a server was very friendly to customers on their last shift but still received low tips. Because of this experience, they conclude that being nice doesn't mean they will receive good tips, and they feel frustrated by this. So the next day, when they serve you, you perceive them as standoffish. The server may not even be consciously aware of how they're coming off, but their new expectation of receiving a small tip influences their behavior toward you. Ultimately, this affects your behavior toward them, causing you to leave them a small tip as they predicted you would.

In this example, how the person treated you directly impacted how you treated them. However, all this happened simply because the server prophesied that they would keep getting small tips based on their experience the previous day. In other words, their belief became true because it affected their behavior toward you. If they had continued their friendly demeanor from the prior day, you would likely have chosen to tip well, ultimately disproving their belief and causing their desired outcome of a good tip. However, their assumption led to a shift in their behavior that *unintentionally* caused an undesirable outcome.

Of course, the server didn't want another small tip, but they accidentally created that reality because their subconscious behaviors increased the likelihood of that happening. From their perspective, you left a small tip because that's what customers do, but in fact, you only left that tip because of their behavior. This is why self-awareness, self-reflection, and thinking in the gray (avoiding black-and-white thinking) are so crucial for all of us; without them, you're at a higher risk of overgeneralizing and creating undesired outcomes by allowing your assumptions to lead to changed behavior that causes the assumption to come true.

Of course, the relationship between someone's expectation of you and your actual behavior is not foolproof. Although someone's expectations can influence your behavior, you, of course, still have free will. Situations won't always play out as I described. For instance, you could be treated rudely and still decide to leave a reasonable tip. Maybe you have a personal rule that you always leave a good tip regardless of the service. The other-imposed self-fulfilling prophecy wouldn't have occurred if this were the case. Instead, it would be a corrective experience for the server since that outcome would challenge their belief that customers always leave poor tips.

Other-imposed self-fulfilling prophecies only happen when our behaviors align with someone else's predictions. The main takeaway is that someone's expectations of us can significantly *increase the likelihood* of us acting according to those expectations, even if we are unaware of them. This happens because their predictions of us influence how they act toward us, which can impact our response.

A very well-known psychology experiment by Dr. Rosenthal & Dr. Jacobson shows just how powerful self-fulfilling prophecies can be.[26] In the study, students were randomly assigned to two groups: the "gifted" group and the "average" group. Again, this was completely random, so in actuality, there were no significant differences between the two groups. The teachers who were part of the experiment were the only ones made aware of what group the students belonged to. The students themselves did not know which group they belonged to or even what the two groups were. Also, the teachers were unaware of the true purpose behind the study, leading them to believe half of their students were gifted and the other half were of average intelligence, even though this was not the case.

When the experimenters later tested the students from both groups, they found the "gifted" group significantly outperformed the "average" group even though there were no significant differences between them at the beginning of the experiment. In other words, the "gifted" group now appeared "gifted" all because the teachers *believed* those students were gifted. Due to their beliefs, the teachers subconsciously treated the "gifted" students differently. They gave the "gifted" students more attention and help, which led to them academically outperforming the other group. Also, because the teachers believed in their abilities, even when the "gifted" students struggled in class, the teachers didn't perceive it as meaning they were less capable. This caused the teachers to have more patience and creativity in helping those students grasp the material. As a result, the teachers did a better job of helping these students reach their full academic potential.

In short, the students became who the teachers believed them to be because the teachers' expectations changed how they treated the students. It didn't even matter that the students didn't know they were part of the "gifted" group. The teachers' expectations of them and subsequent change in behavior toward them were all that was needed for the other-imposed self-fulfilling prophecy to occur.

Studies like this one help us grasp just how influential and powerful our beliefs can be when it comes to the behaviors of others and the outcomes of situations. Labeling someone can lead to the person displaying behaviors that match the label. If this can happen even when a person is unaware of the label, imagine how much more influential a label can be when they are aware of it.

Think about how you were labeled in your family as you were growing up or maybe even how you refer to your own children if you have them. Perhaps you were labeled a "troublemaker," which caused your parents to have less patience for your mistakes and rarely give you the benefit of the doubt. Or perhaps you were labeled "the smart one," which caused you to become a perfectionist and to feel intense shame when you didn't perform as well as you hoped despite that being an occasional inevitability.

The powerful impact that our beliefs can have on our behaviors and emotions is also why I personally choose not to refer to my two-year-old's current stage of life as the "terrible twos." Scientifically, I know that these behaviors are developmentally expected and normal for his age and limited skill set. This is also why all toddler parents can relate to one another's experiences; two-year-olds act like two-year-olds, and that's just a fact. Expecting them to be any different when they haven't even had sufficient time to learn from us (because learning happens slowly over time) and while their brains are still so under-developed is unreasonable and even impossible. Again, expecting my two-year-old son to be able to regulate his emotions *consistently* or even *frequently* is the equivalent of me expecting him to know how to do calculus. Developmentally, he is not yet able to do such a thing consistently because of how the brain develops over time. Plus, as his parents, it is our responsibility to teach him this invaluable skill through co-regulation. As time goes on, we are seeing this skill develop as he gets better and better at doing so with our guidance and through practice.

Refraining from encouraging this mentality keeps me empathetic, patient, and mindful of my responsibility to teach him skills and guide him based on his current developmental needs. Remember, learning requires consistency, repetition, explanation, modeling, creativity, and reasonable expectations of change. Referring to him as "bad," especially frequently, could (and likely would) subconsciously alter my behavior and emotions in a negative way that would negatively impact my parenting. It also would negatively affect his self-esteem and would be me blaming him instead of being accountable for my obligation to regulate myself while teaching him.

Parenting is already a massive job that has the potential to dysregulate us, and I wouldn't want to add difficulty by choosing to nurture a perspective that has the potential to make things worse. The potential consequences are not worth the risk, so I choose to process any challenging experiences with my son through the lens of what is developmentally expected and needed, which helps guide me in my parenting and healthy discipline. As a result, he learns more quickly and efficiently. This also benefits me with my own emotional regulation because I have empathy and an accurate perspective of these experiences.

Thinking about the power of your beliefs and their influence over you and others can help you be mindful of avoiding harmful or undesired outcomes. It brings to your attention that your mindset may be the most significant contributor to why things happen that you wish wouldn't occur as often or at all. If you are willing to shift your mindset, expectations, and behaviors, you may find that people are capable of things you thought they weren't and, in some cases, that they change more quickly. You may also find you are capable of more than you believed you were too.

Plus, doing so helps you rule yourself out when it comes to *adult* interactions and relationships. Suppose you know that you are consistently showing up in a reasonable, empathetic manner and being mindful of your actions and words. In that case, this helps you more easily identify adults in your life who are unwilling to do the same. You will be able to determine relationships that are unhealthy for you, and you will confidently know that it's not due to a negative self-fulfilling prophecy (as long as you are also mindful of your human biases). In other words, it's not your behaviors or expectations that are influencing the other adult's poor behaviors; instead, it is their relationship with themselves and simply a reflection of their internal struggles.

Another important lesson from this is that labels and absolute language (like always, never, every, etc.) usually cannot account for the complexity of situations or a person. Outcomes typically depend on a multitude of factors, so when we have hard, fast, inflexible rules, we often do more damage to ourselves and others than we do good. Just like the example of the server assuming *all* customers are poor tippers and being friendly *never* makes a difference. Life experiences are too nuanced to be oversimplified that way because absolute language fails to account for the various factors in each individual situation that have the potential to impact the final outcome.

Now, to be clear, we should *absolutely* observe a person's patterns of behavior to make decisions about the relationships we choose for our lives. For example, if someone has a pattern of severely mistreating you, this should be heavily weighed when deciding on the longevity of that relationship. Still, the complex nature of that person as a whole likely cannot be summed up using absolutes. If we are deliberate in our use of words based on their meaning, there are only a handful of things that a person *always* does (like I am always breathing, for instance). Even if they frequently mistreat you, you can probably also think of times when they didn't. Regardless, the concerning existence of the pattern in the first place is what matters most and outweighs any kind acts they might occasionally do. In other words, it doesn't matter that they don't *always* mistreat you because the chronic pattern of bad behavior is enough reason to consider ending the relationship, despite the fact that they can sometimes be nice too. Since absolutes rarely fit, we have to make decisions based on whether the bad outweighs the good.

Self-Imposed Self-Fulfilling Prophecies

A self-imposed prophecy is when your beliefs directly affect you and your outcomes. Specifically, it's when you have an expectation (or essentially make a prediction) that comes true. Again, this occurs because merely having the expectation can cause you to subconsciously change your behavior in a way that aligns with your prediction. If you don't analyze the situation, you're left believing your prediction was right in the first place. You don't realize your behaviors led to the belief coming true. You prove yourself "right" by doing things that cause your prediction to come true, but if you hadn't, an outcome that would have contradicted your prediction was also very possible.

A relatable example where this can occur is a pattern of failed relationships. Of course, there are numerous reasons why a pattern like this can form, but one common explanation is self-imposed self-fulfilling prophecies. Let's say you expect your romantic relationships are doomed to fail. You may make this prediction for several reasons. Maybe people in your life have struggled to find and form healthy, happy relationships, or perhaps you recently had a failed relationship yourself. Regardless of how this expectation developed, your choices can ultimately make your prediction come true.

You might subconsciously sabotage your chances of a healthy relationship by continuously getting into relationships with partners who have very similar qualities. Essentially, you would end up dating the same kind of person over and over, which would lead to multiple failed relationships. Unfortunately, each experience would only reinforce your belief that all your relationships will fail, and the stronger that belief becomes, the more likely it would be that you will have the same outcome. It would become a vicious cycle because you never thoroughly processed and addressed the root issue, your choice of partner.

Again, failed relationships happen due to a combination of factors, including an attraction to the familiar, problematic behaviors we need to improve in ourselves and the current shortage of healthy potential partners who are dedicated to caring for their mental health. Still, self-imposed prophecies are a prevalent cause of patterns like this.

And even in situations with other contributing factors, self-imposed self-fulfilling prophecies often still play a significant role.

On the other hand, if you recognized the pattern of failed relationships as an opportunity for self-exploration and reflection, you could avoid falling prey to a self-fulfilling prophecy. When you see a pattern occurring in your life, you should be curious about why it is happening and identify what's in your control and what you need to change.

As I briefly shared earlier, before meeting my husband, I was in an emotionally and psychologically abusive relationship for over three years. I also had other failed relationships before that one. I truly loved that ex during our relationship, even though he could not love me the way I deserved. He had a significant trauma history that he never acknowledged, and he rarely engaged in meaningful self-reflection. His mindset was, "I am who I am. Love it or leave it." Also, because of the toxic beliefs he was taught about his emotions, masculinity, and mental health, he was unwilling to accept that certain experiences had harmed him psychologically, behaviorally, and emotionally.

All the signs were there early on that this would not be a healthy relationship for me, but at the time, my unresolved trauma caused me to proceed anyway; I mistakenly gave him the benefit of the doubt too many times and went against my best judgment. When I confronted him about my concerns, he always found a way to gaslight me or convince me that it wouldn't happen again. I now know a relationship starting so poorly is a massive red flag, but I didn't realize it then. Instead, I allowed the fact that I wanted the relationship to work to stop me from accepting reality. From there, an addictive cycle was created. I experienced many "good" moments that felt loving and drew me deeper into the relationship. Still, I also dealt with his frequent lies and cheating and instances of him feeding my insecurities, which lowered my self-esteem.

I eventually decided to leave the relationship because it was toxic to my mental health and hindered my growth. After ending the relationship, I went to therapy for the first time. I wanted to understand my mentality and how my trauma led me to choose him as a partner. I also wanted to understand what being in that relationship had done to me psychologically so I could begin healing. My main goal was to understand why I chose to stay for three years so I would never make that choice again with anyone else like him.

My decision to seek help allowed me to break my cycle of self-imposed self-fulfilling prophecies. I discovered I had a belief about myself that I could change people if I just loved them hard enough, but in reality, that is not how things work. That belief (amongst others) caused me to choose partners who weren't healthy for me, and I accidentally created a pattern of failed relationships. I now know that because of free will, people must decide to do the work to change themselves, and the only person I can ever change is me. The most I can do for someone else is attempt to support them while they change, but it is ultimately up to them to decide to do the work. I can't do it for them, and I can't make them do it, no matter how much I love them. Therapy helped me discover the many things leading to my self-imposed self-fulfilling prophecies, allowing me to heal.

The self-work I did at the time helped me later find and marry my soulmate because I began dating differently. If I hadn't unlearned those beliefs, I would have been stuck in a cycle of dating the same type of person and experiencing more failed relationships. In short, my unresolved trauma had attracted me to toxicity and caused me to overlook what was truly healthy. Plus, at the time, there was knowledge that I did not have about human behavior and how change truly works, which I needed in order to break this mentality.

Because of all the childhood trauma and poor parenting that has led to the high rates of mental health concerns in adults, dating is definitely more challenging than it was ever meant to be. However, I realized the only thing in my control to make my odds of finding healthy love better was to do the work to become healthier myself.

I needed to educate myself, change my mentality, and work on my behaviors in order to be able to identify and appreciate a healthy relationship. This is what gave me better odds, despite the challenges that neglecting mental health has created within society, and thankfully, I was able to find a healthy, compatible partner. If I hadn't done the work, he would have been found and chosen by someone else who had.

If someone else's beliefs about us have the power to influence how we act, it makes sense that our own beliefs about ourselves can do the same. Our thoughts about ourselves often have even more influence because we are always with our thoughts. Since we can't escape them, we must be mindful of them and, when necessary, correct them so their influence on us is positive.

Let's look at some important takeaways to help you protect yourself and use self-fulfilling prophecies to your advantage.

Understanding self-fulfilling prophecies is how you protect yourself. I've said it once and will say it again: knowledge is power! By understanding how self-fulfilling prophecies work, you can increase your self-awareness, which helps you remain mindful of your assumptions and their impact on your behaviors. By being more aware, you can decrease the likelihood of putting yourself in avoidable harmful situations and sharpen your critical thinking skills.

The main reason negative self-fulfilling prophecies happen is that this phenomenon is still not common knowledge, which has unfortunately led to it being a common practice. If you don't know what something is, it's tough to detect what's happening and why, just like it's hard to recognize when you're being gaslit until someone explains gaslighting to you. Learning about things and having a name for them helps you identify when that thing is happening and enables you to determine changes you can make to break the cycle.

Next time you find yourself in a pattern, check in with your thoughts. Have you made any assumptions that are impacting your behaviors? If so, change your behavior and see how this affects the outcome. Changing your behavior once and having the same result is not always enough proof that your original belief was correct, so it's also essential to be reasonable. *Consistent* changes in our behavior help us see if doing so leads to different outcomes since there are usually other factors that impact how a situation goes. In other words, other explanations exist for why your changes may not immediately lead to a different result. For instance, if you change your dating habits, it's still possible a new relationship may not work. Perhaps you overlooked a major compatibility issue, causing the relationship to fail. Either way, you can remove self-fulfilling prophecies from the equation by being mindful of your assumptions, which can make the dating process a bit more straightforward (because your unhelpful beliefs will no longer subconsciously cloud your judgment, making it easier to see a person for who they are).

Yes, of course, dating will still be a bit complicated. Still, by not creating a negative self-fulfilling prophecy, you can increase self-awareness and decrease the likelihood of unintentional self-sabotage.

Use this knowledge to create positive self-fulfilling prophecies. After I learned about self-fulfilling prophecies, I started using my thoughts to influence my life positively. Since our thoughts are essentially the starting point for specific outcomes, you can choose thoughts that encourage positive outcomes. Of course, it won't always work out because there are other factors, but what is for sure is that negative assumptions significantly decrease how often you have positive experiences. In other words, when you allow yourself to have fewer negative assumptions, you increase the *likelihood* of having more positive experiences.

Because of my trauma, for the longest, I immediately assumed the worst of others. Generalizing was a trauma response meant to protect me from hurt, and many times it did, but the problem was it also prevented me from receiving more positive experiences. The default assumptions I had at the time were too extreme. I was creating other-imposed self-fulfilling prophecies without realizing it, which negatively impacted my interactions with people and caused me to miss out on good relationships.

Once I learned how self-fulfilling prophecies worked, I used them to my advantage. For example, I predicted a new experience would be enjoyable or at least beneficial in some way. When you go into a new situation assuming the worst, you prime yourself to make that situation unenjoyable. Imagine going to a social event. If you go into that situation with the mindset that no one will like you, it will affect your behavior. You'll be less likely to engage with people and may even come across as standoffish to "protect" yourself from rejection. That's what I used to do before I realized what I was doing. The problem is these behaviors guarantee rejection and create an other-imposed self-fulfilling prophecy.

Going to an event with a cautiously hopeful and open-minded mindset would lead to very different behaviors. Maybe you still won't end up meeting anyone at the event who you'd like to build a friendship with, but at least you can be sure this outcome won't be due to your behavior. You can leave the event saying, "Hey! I was friendly and had some good conversations. I was genuinely myself and gave people a real chance, but I just didn't click on a deeper level with anyone. Sure, it's disappointing, but I still had a good time, and maybe next time I'll really connect with someone!"

This mindset is encouraging, so you will be more likely to keep connecting with new people, only increasing the likelihood of finding a quality friendship soon enough. Finding good, authentic relationships is a trial-and-error process for us all. You may need time after the social event before you're ready to try again, but your improved mindset will keep you encouraged. Since finding good relationships takes time, it's so important not to add to the difficulty by causing negative self-fulfilling prophecies through your mindset and behaviors.

Of course, there are times when making a negative assumption is well-founded, so it's important to have discernment and nurture your critical thinking skills. A "better safe than sorry" approach is always best if something genuinely seems sketchy or if it's just not worth the risk. More than anything, this is about learning to trust yourself and your judgment without getting in your own way. When it's safe to do so, allow yourself to cautiously assume the best, not the worst, and see how things play out for you. It's impossible to completely avoid undesirable situations, but you can avoid being the *cause* of the negativity and use your free will to remove yourself from situations when needed.

Be mindful of your trauma's role. As I shared with the examples throughout this chapter, trauma often plays a significant role in self-fulfilling prophecies. Give yourself grace when you're unlearning certain thought patterns. Many are attached to traumatic experiences, so the fact that you adopted these beliefs to protect yourself is understandable.

When you're working on healing, you must let go of thoughts and behaviors that may have been protective in the past but are now preventing your growth. Holding on to them can often cause you to miss out on opportunities, like new healthy relationships and experiences. Allowing your trauma responses to trap you in a cycle of self-fulfilling prophecies deprives you of corrective experiences and healing. Unlearning these trauma responses is how you regain control over the trajectory of your life.

More than likely, your new, healthier mindset will fall into the "gray" instead of the "black-and-white" beliefs that trauma often causes us to develop. So, instead of having a "black-and-white" belief that *all* people will mistreat or use you, as you begin to heal, you will develop a mindset that *some* people frequently engage in those types of harmful behaviors. You will accept that the knowledge you are gaining from outside sources and from critically thinking about your experiences is what will help you identify and avoid those types of people. You will realize that educating yourself is how you can become more trusting of your decision-making abilities. You will begin to understand that observing patterns of behavior is the best way to protect yourself and that the "black-and-white" thinking would prevent you from connecting with the kinds of people you desire to meet and that do exist! In summary, you will develop more of a "gray" or flexible way of seeing life that allows you to acknowledge its complexity, avoid inaccurate absolutes, and significantly decrease the likelihood of unwanted self-fulfilling prophecies.

One thing is clear: the effects of trauma are complicated and multifaceted. But if you commit to raising your self-awareness, you can identify the effects, heal, and grow. My hope for you and me is that we will never forget just how precious making this commitment is. The greatest thing about evolving is that there isn't a limit unless we decide to set one. Humans are complex, so there are endless ways to improve ourselves.

I wish there was a quick fix, but there isn't. Healing is a process, and the first step is equipping yourself with knowledge while being committed and intentional about how you respond to your human experiences. I pray you will not embark on this journey alone. It's best to seek support from people who can genuinely help you grow. Reading this book is already a commitment to not doing it alone because help from others comes in many forms. Continuing to learn about psychology and mental health will also be useful throughout your journey. In this day and age, you have unlimited access to free information and resources; use that to your advantage. Just make sure this information is coming from reputable sources by fact-checking because there is misleading information out there as well.

If you are doing it right, your growth will happen in stages and be lifelong, so celebrate each step of the journey as you continue to push forward! Engage in positive self-fulfilling prophecies often, and do all you can to avoid negative ones like they are the plague (because they pretty much are.) You deserve not to get in the way of your blessings simply because you don't recognize your own patterns. Honest self-analysis and critically thinking about your experiences will help you better understand your role and the role of others, leading to a healthier, more accurate view of what is occurring and why.

CHAPTER 8

The Distorted Mind

Beware your thoughts so you can be aware of them.

Our minds can play tricks on us; after all, if other people can manipulate us, of course, we can occasionally mislead ourselves too. However, educating ourselves on the psychology of thought errors can help us decrease this habit by increasing our self-awareness. These errors of thought are commonly referred to as cognitive distortions.

When I first learned about cognitive distortions, it changed my life. Like in a video game, this knowledge unlocked a new ability. Not having a name for our experiences prevents us from breaking bad habits or fully recognizing how those habits impact our lives. However, when we can name something for what it is, we can identify it, and when we can identify it, we can also correct it. Think about it. Before someone taught you the difference between a truth and a lie, you didn't know what a lie was. The same is true for everything you know.

Psychology gives us an in-depth understanding of our thoughts, emotions, and behaviors so we can become excellent managers of self. Without that knowledge, life is more chaotic because we don't have an effective way to self-analyze. When we lack the language to identify the types of thoughts we're having, label what we're feeling, and describe precisely what we're doing, it's harder to determine what we need to change and why. And even when we can identify it, we still may not know how to change it. Psychology gives us the invaluable gift of understanding *why* we do what we do, *what* we need to change, and *how* we can change it, allowing us to better navigate our lives and monitor ourselves.

In psychology, cognitive distortions are part of *what* needs to be changed. This chapter will define these mental slip-ups and how to respond when they occur. You're likely familiar with most of them because we're all guilty of thinking this way. However, many of us lack a way to label these experiences, which makes it challenging to recognize how problematic and counterproductive they can be. Even though irrational thoughts are a normal part of the human experience, we don't have to allow them to negatively impact our lives.

Once you understand how these thoughts shape your perspective, you will have the power of discernment. Awareness allows you to make an educated choice. After identifying a cognitive distortion, you can choose to reframe and correct it—and I hope you do! Thoughts are powerless until you decide to breathe life into them. Ultimately, it is up to you which thoughts you choose to nurture and which you choose to correct.

So, what are cognitive distortions?

"Cognitive" refers to our thoughts, and "distortions" refers to errors, so essentially, cognitive distortions are thought errors or, in other words, irrational thoughts. They happen to varying degrees and can distort your reality, so the consequences of fueling these thoughts can be costly. There are many types of cognitive distortions.

For the sake of this chapter, I will thoroughly cover some of the most common ones as well as techniques I use with clients to help them correct these thoughts when necessary. Also, I hope you will seek out information on other types of cognitive distortions so you can expand your understanding and vocabulary beyond the ones that I was able to cover in this chapter.

Emotional Reasoning

In my professional experience, emotional reasoning is a cognitive distortion that many people frequently struggle with, especially if they are not aware of what they are doing. It's also the one I used to be most guilty of (and because of this, I remain mindful of avoiding it as much as possible). Simply put, this is when we assume our emotions *always* represent how life is. The problem is that we fail to consider other evidence or information when we reason this way.

Here are some examples of emotional reasoning:

- "I feel like I burden everyone, so I don't want to burden them more by discussing my problems."
- "I think they're mad at me. I must have done something wrong."
- "I feel so stupid. I'm an idiot!"
- "I feel worthless. I can't do anything right."
- "It feels like no one could ever love me, so I guess I'll be alone forever."

The main reason many of us fall into the trap of emotional reasoning is because our emotions do communicate valuable information. But just like in the game of telephone, we sometimes fail to interpret the message accurately. When we have an emotional shift, we are supposed to acknowledge and process what we're feeling. However, in many cases, we can't use that information alone to process a situation accurately. Our feelings provide vital information, but they are not the *only* information we should consider.

I'm sure you can think of many scenarios where you relied on your gut, and you were right. But it's also important to acknowledge the other times when you felt just as certain and ended up being wrong. Your emotional reactions are not foolproof because they depend on how you interpret the situation (your thoughts). If your initial assumption is faulty, your emotional response is then based on faulty judgment. In other words, although they are separate things, your interpretation of what occurred is the foundation upon which your emotions are built. You can avoid emotional reasoning by being mindful of the source of your emotional reaction. Doing so is vital because how you choose to respond (your behaviors) often depends on how you feel.

I bet you've heard people say they use rationality to make decisions instead of emotionality. I've always found this funny because rationality and emotionality naturally work together due to brain anatomy. Your frontal lobe, the largest lobe of the brain and considered the emotional and behavioral control center, is responsible for your personality, impulse control, problem-solving, emotional responses, behaviors, and more. Not only that, but all four lobes of the brain have parts that serve some type of emotion-related function. Basically, your brain is one big emotional organ (with many other vital functions, of course)

Because of this, you're always in an emotional state of some kind, whether you realize it or not, so emotions play a role even when you're reasoning. As stated earlier, your thoughts influence your feelings, regardless of whether the thoughts are rational or irrational. Of course, you can have an *irrational* thought that leads to specific emotions but still decide to engage in a *rational* behavioral response. However, this would still be representative of these three systems sharing a relationship. In other words, you realize you are at risk of engaging in an irrational behavior based on unreasonable *thoughts*, which you then *feel* is not the right way to handle things, so you think of a different response and choose a different *behavior*.

Just because self-awareness and free will help you in these types of situations doesn't mean you made a behavioral decision that was *completely* independent of emotion. You likely had separate emotions when you realized the original thought was irrational, which led to you changing your mindset and, subsequently, your behavior. My point is there's no way to pull them apart completely because they are all a part of an interconnected system within your brain. When it comes to your emotional experiences, your job is to analyze the thoughts that are the source of those feelings. This is how you determine the best way to respond to the situation and how to best meet your emotional needs.

Automatic & Intrusive Thoughts

In a day, we can have up to 60,000 thoughts, most of them repetitive. Thankfully, we sift through many of them without an issue, and others, we don't pay much attention to. But with all those thoughts, it's unsurprising that we sometimes misinterpret our environment, focus on the wrong details, and accidentally encourage irrational thoughts.

We all experience automatic thoughts, but that doesn't mean we have to function on autopilot. When we practice appropriately responding to these thoughts, we maintain a healthy level of control over our experiences. Automatic thoughts are normal, but they frequently need to be challenged to prevent them from taking over. We sometimes forget our ability to respond to them, especially when they're overwhelming or unpleasant. We have to remember we have a responsibility to analyze and correct them when needed; not doing so can be problematic for our lives and our mental health.

I know it can sometimes feel like having certain thoughts is the be-all and end-all, but thankfully, it's not! Despite the emotional distress they can sometimes cause, thoughts only have the power you give them. When you do not filter them, you allow your thoughts to control you instead of you controlling them. Since having thoughts is an inevitable part of the human experience, don't waste your energy trying not to have them. Instead, focus your energy on responding to the thoughts that require a response and dismissing the ones that do not serve you. Of course, this takes practice because it's a skill. But when you accept that constantly having thoughts is simply part of the human experience, it helps you accept that their existence is not a cause for alarm. You get to decide which thoughts you focus on and respond to.

Remember: you are in charge of your mind; your mind isn't in charge of you. Your job is to notice and sift through the information you receive. Then, respond in a healthy, emotionally informed, and rational way, a skill you can continually improve with deliberate and conscious practice.

Now, this doesn't mean you shouldn't acknowledge the emotions your distressing thoughts cause. You should never ignore your feelings because they don't just magically go away. You need to tend to them so you can move through what you feel and release it. The goal is to accept your feelings while also responding to and, when needed, correcting your thoughts. It doesn't have to be one or the other. You can and should do both! Even if you realize your feelings are based on an irrational thought, it's still important to acknowledge the distress the thought caused if you felt any. Once the emotion exists, you must work through it if you don't want to hold on to it. That's the healthiest, most effective way to respond to all your needs. This approach covers all bases.

Some of your automatic thoughts are neutral and don't affect you much, such as when you think, "Hmm, it's warm today," as you step outside. However, automatic *intrusive* thoughts tend to be the most challenging to navigate, and understandably so. Have you ever walked into a bank and noticed the idea of what it would be like to rob it pop into your head out of nowhere? Have you ever been in a good mood and, all of a sudden, thought about something terrible happening to a loved one? Those are intrusive thoughts, and although they can be very distressing, you must remind yourself that they are normal. Having them from time to time is out of your control, but how you respond to them is not.

If you worry that the innocent, random thought means you actually want to rob the bank or that something terrible is about to happen to your loved one, then that will cause you distress. But reminding yourself that intrusive thoughts are automatic and something we all experience will help you decrease your distress. That way, you won't accidentally make things worse by giving them more meaning than they have.

The thought alone is distressing enough, so don't feed into it more. Instead, just respond to the thought by labeling it as intrusive and grounding yourself in the fact that it has no significance in your actual life. It's just one of those 60,000 thoughts that float into your head on a given day, and it doesn't determine anything unless you allow it to.

Your brain is basically a machine. A machine is any physical system capable of performing certain functions, and thinking is one of many functions your brain can perform. As with any machine, glitches are not only a possibility but an inevitability, and intrusive thoughts are glitches of the mind. They are entirely meaningless and should be treated as such. They're just a weird part of the human experience that you don't want to overthink or encourage in any way. The healthiest way to deal with intrusive thoughts after noticing them is to let them float away and then move on to a thought of your *choice* (since you don't choose intrusive thoughts). Think of them as uninvited guests, and kick them out of the party that is your mind as quickly as you can because they don't belong there.

You'll likely find it easiest to quickly dismiss intrusive thoughts that don't feel very personal, such as the bank robbery example. It's easier to ignore and rarely, if ever, causes us emotional distress because your follow-up (chosen) thoughts are usually about the fact that you know the idea is ridiculous. You know you don't desire to rob anybody, let alone a whole bank. (Although it would be cool if they decided to award you money for being the hundredth customer of the day!) Because of this, it's easy to ground yourself in your values and character and use that to move past the thought like it never happened. Seconds later, you've made your deposit and are on your way to running your next errand.

However, when an intrusive thought relates to an actual fear you may have, such as losing a loved one, sometimes ignoring it doesn't feel like enough. Since it feels personal, you may feel compelled to fixate on it. None of us enjoy unpleasant thoughts about things or people that mean a lot to us, no matter how short-lived the thought might be. However, the thought alone does not represent or determine what will occur. It's a manifestation of your worries, not a prediction of the future. These thoughts often happen in response to stress and anxiety, and reminding yourself of their source can help you move *through* the feelings. Nonetheless, it can help to have other ways to process and respond when ignoring the thought or letting it pass doesn't immediately work.

Maybe you recently heard about someone losing a family member, perhaps from a true crime show or social media, and that primed you to think about the mortality of your loved ones. In this case, it would be helpful to remind yourself that worrying about your loved ones after hearing about someone else's loss is normal and even expected, but it doesn't mean you are about to lose anyone.

Or maybe the thought popped into your head because you're still actively grieving the loss of a different family member. In this case, it would be helpful to remind yourself that grief can often come in waves and then take time to reflect on the loss and process any emotions that resurface. Either way, the intrusive thought itself still has no real significance and tells you nothing about how much time you have left with your living loved ones. Channel that distressing energy and use it as a motivator to connect more with anybody you're worried about losing. Doing so can help ease some of the distress and help you move past the irrelevant intrusive thoughts.

Here are a few ways to connect with a loved one:

- Say what you most want to tell them.
- Remind the person how much they mean to you.
- Talk to them about your fear of losing them so you can emotionally support and connect with one another to work through the distressing thoughts together.
- Write them a heartfelt letter or make some other gesture of affection.
- Plan a visit or an outing to spend quality time together.
- Video chat with the person and catch up.

Taking these kinds of actions in response to the anxiety can help you shift your focus back to the beauty of your connection with this person instead of your fear of losing them one day. You don't know the future or control how much time you have with anyone, but you absolutely control how you spend that time. As you learned in Chapter 3, anxiety is a call to action. It's your brain's way of grabbing your attention so you can either do or say something to improve a situation. In this case, the call to action is for connection. By seeking contact with the person, you can move through the anxiety and experience positive emotions that help you combat the anxiety that the intrusive thought caused.

Remember your follow-up thoughts (the ones you choose with intention) can either be the extinguisher that puts out the fire or the gas that accelerates it. That depends on how you choose to respond. Think of the thoughts you choose as your best defense against those you don't choose. When honed, this superpower can significantly improve your ability to effectively manage your mind! I know these thoughts can be upsetting, but remind yourself that what you choose to think after provides you with an opportunity to move past intrusive thoughts.

When I have particularly upsetting intrusive thoughts, my favorite way to shift my mindset is to say, "No!" in a commanding voice in my head or, better yet, aloud. I usually choose to say it aloud (even if I need to say it softly) because it feels more powerful. I say, "Nope! Uh-uh, brain. We are not doing this today!" I also label the thought and talk through it to ground myself. I might say, "That was an intrusive thought! It has no power over me. I have been feeling stressed today, so it makes sense that it happened. I also love and care about that person a lot, so that intrusive thought simply represents my anxiety about never wanting anything to happen to them, but nothing is happening. They are just fine, and everything is okay! We all worry about things like that from time to time. It's normal, and it means nothing." Talking myself through it helps me ground myself back in reality and get out of my head.

When intrusive thoughts grab your attention and upset you, respond and talk yourself through them. It may take some time, and you may even need support from others, but that's okay! We all need support from others, and we are supposed to allow ourselves to seek help as often as needed for challenges, both big and small. We were all designed to be so emotionally hardwired because we were biologically intended to carry the weight of our intense emotional experiences together, both positive and negative. This is, again, why empathy is a skill that *all* humans need to learn and embody. Too often, because of the stigma around mental health and people being misinformed about human needs, we fail to do this and instead suffer in isolation, which is not how things were meant to be. Healing this dangerous and unhealthy pattern of human behavior is the key to the rates of mental health disorders drastically dropping. Once we heal and allow our day-to-day interactions to be what they were *actually* meant to be (emotionally intimate), we will all *finally* begin to care for each other properly according to how we were designed.

Remind yourself that everything is fine as much and as often as needed. The thought will pass with time and from you actively responding to it through self-talk and, when needed, action, like seeking support. As with any skill, it takes practice and trial and error, but with time, you can find what works best for you during moments like this, just as I have.

As discussed earlier, please don't hesitate to get creative! When working on your personal growth, meet yourself where you are; doing so is the only way to get to where you want to be. This often requires coming up with creative ideas that help you step out of your comfort zone while also allowing you to meet your emotional needs, as some distress is typically part of the process. Feeling silly, anxious, or uncomfortable is normal when learning new skills, especially emotional and behavioral management skills. Embrace whatever feelings you have and recognize they are a good sign! After all, you're doing something new to improve how you address a need, and those emotions confirm that you're challenging yourself and moving out of your comfort zone so you can grow. Remember: your emotions aren't something to fear. Embrace them.

Don't allow feeling silly to stop you from fulfilling your personal development goals. Silliness is a small price to pay for your overall well-being. Allow yourself to feel silly so you can learn or relearn how to work with this emotion. As a child, there was a reason you allowed yourself to feel freely and didn't mind looking or being silly. You're supposed to feel and work with your feelings; this is the foundation of your personal development. Retrain your nervous system by improving your self-talk and your behavioral responses to your emotions so you no longer see silliness or embarrassment as a threat. If you allow yourself to sit with them, especially when it leads to self-improvement, you will gain a new appreciation for them over time. Doing so has led to this appreciation for me.

The Rabbit Hole

I often use a "rabbit hole" analogy to help my clients practice moving through and past distressing thoughts. In this analogy, the intrusive automatic thought is the rabbit hole. When you realize one of these thoughts has crossed your mind, you have an immediate decision to make. You can either dive into the hole headfirst or start filling it so you don't fall in. This depends on the quality of your follow-up chosen thoughts. In other words, how you *choose* to respond to the automatic thought itself. If you don't want to give the automatic thought power over you, then the decision is simple: you must choose to fill the hole.

Here's an example of what filling the hole looks like. Let's imagine you're struggling with low self-esteem because of bullying experiences that you haven't emotionally recovered from yet. Then you're introduced to someone new, and the automatic thought, "This person isn't going to like me," pops into your head within seconds. Left unchecked, that belief will cause negative emotions and affect your behaviors and interactions with this new person. This is the consequence of diving into the hole. Before the person even learns your name, you're already at the dangerous start of a negative self-fulfilling prophecy, and as you learned earlier, if you aren't mindful, your negative beliefs can quickly become your reality.

Now, having the automatic thought, considering your past experiences, isn't surprising. It's understandable; bullying takes a toll on your self-confidence, but failing to correct these thoughts leaves you continuing the work your bullies started. They're long gone, but their negative influence continues through your self-talk. It's as if you signed up for the position after they retired from it.

Even when your brain isn't being very helpful, it usually has good intentions. When we have had adverse experiences in the past, our brains will begin to respond differently to new experiences to try to protect us from more pain. After all, in this case, the automatic thought was an attempt to protect yourself from the rejection you've experienced in the past. But the problem is that this particular thought is too definitive, considering you barely interacted with the person.

Suppose you fail to analyze and replace this thought with a chosen thought that better reflects the situation. In that case, you will accidentally engage in two cognitive distortions: fortune telling (expecting circumstances to turn out badly without adequate evidence) and emotional reasoning (assuming your emotions *always* reflect the way things really are). Failing to respond well to this automatic thought would cause you to reject yourself before the new person has even gotten a chance to know you. Instead of protecting yourself, you make a premature assumption based on a story you are telling yourself in your head, and this prevents you from seeing what could be. As a result, you would feel rejected, but that emotion would be a product of the automatic thought itself and not because the person actually rejected you.

There was a time when you didn't automatically assume a new person wouldn't like you, so now that the damage is done, how will you get back to that version of yourself? That's where filling the hole serves you best. By practicing this skill, you choose to take the damaged pieces of your confidence and use them to construct a stronger structure than the one you began with when the trauma occurred.

Change and healing are active and deliberate processes. They don't just magically occur no matter how good your intentions or the strength of your desire for them, although, of course, these are helpful motivators. Instead, you receive change and healing as the rewards for your hard work and dedication. They're like a paycheck at the end of a long workweek, and the only way to earn them is to do the work.

If you choose to fill the rabbit hole, the first step is to catch yourself and label the intrusive thought through your self-talk. Even though it may feel obvious, it's also *necessary* to specifically remind yourself how this thought relates to your trauma. This raises your self-awareness and allows you to consciously process what is occurring and why. Doing so is part of grounding yourself and finding your footing, which protects you from falling into the hole.

Next, practice responding to the thought instead of egging it on. Responding allows you to take the grounding step further while simultaneously acknowledging your feelings. When you egg the thought on, you ground yourself in your mind (instead of in reality) and accidentally add to your distress. You allow the intrusive thought to be taken as fact without substantial evidence. The truth of this scenario is that the person doesn't know you and has no reason to dislike you. Sure, your past experiences are one form of evidence, but this new person has absolutely nothing to do with the people who bullied you. This person doesn't even know the people who bullied you. Plus, because of human bias, many of your "rejection" experiences *after* you were bullied could have been the result of negative self-fulfilling prophecies created by your belief's influence on your behaviors.

If anything, your life has shown you people can like *or* dislike you, sometimes with very little justification either way (such as when you like someone you've just met because you find them attractive). People can also be nice or mean. People can be rational or irrational. People are complex, unique individuals with multiple factors that shape who they are and how they behave toward you. So jumping to conclusions about everyone you meet will not serve you well, no matter your past experiences. Forming conclusions only serves you well once you've gone beyond your instantaneous impressions, checked your own biases, and reflected on the quality of your behaviors and the behavioral patterns of others.

With everything following the ellipses representing controlled, chosen thoughts, here's an example of egging the thought on: *This person isn't going to like me . . . OMG, of course, they won't! I'm always so awkward when meeting new people. They're going to think I'm weird. Ugh! Why would they like me? Who would ever like me?*

With everything following the ellipses representing controlled, chosen thoughts, here's an example of responding to the thought: *This person isn't going to like me . . . Wait. No, I don't know that. I'm worried about that, but I don't know for sure. I tend to be hard on myself when I meet new people because it makes me nervous. Let me just focus on being myself and see what happens. If I get rejected, it just means this isn't someone I connect with, and that's okay. We're all different people, and my job is to find people I vibe well with.*

It's apparent how the first example of egging the intrusive thought on would make you feel worse and ruin the interaction before it began. It pulls you deeper into the rabbit hole. And trust me, you don't want to go down there. There's nothing down the rabbit hole except more distress, and you don't need more; the intrusive thought is distressing enough.

In contrast, responding fills the hole with rationality and validation. The second example models accepting and acknowledging your feelings while also preventing cognitive distortion. Responding to your emotions allows you to acknowledge your fear of rejection without allowing it to ruin the interaction from the jump. How you talk yourself *through* the thought helps you recover from it. You don't want to gaslight yourself by invalidating your emotions, but you also don't want to upset yourself more unintentionally. Instead, choose to add dirt to the hole with every follow-up (chosen) thought, and eventually, you'll fill the hole. Plus, as time goes on, similar intrusive thoughts will need less dirt for you to move past them because you'll get better at this skill.

Simply put, egging it on is emotional reasoning, telling yourself you feel this way, so it must be true. This isn't necessarily the case. As I explained earlier in the chapter, you can feel a certain way and be wrong. How often have you assumed something only to find out you were wrong? I don't know about you, but that has happened many times throughout my life. I assumed someone was mad at me who wasn't, or I randomly felt anxious and thought something bad would happen, but it didn't.

Again, your emotions are very useful but not foolproof; to avoid emotional reasoning, you have to analyze your thoughts and any other relevant information. A simple way to determine if your emotional reaction is based on rational or irrational thought is to ask yourself: "What evidence do I have to support this thought?" If your feelings are your *only* evidence, then there's a higher risk that those emotions result from an irrational thought. Of course, even if this is the case, your feelings still matter, but you must acknowledge that choosing to shift to and nurture a healthier mindset would change how you feel.

When you use your emotions alone to justify a belief, it's like explaining something with "Because I said so!" You have to check in with yourself and see whether you find more evidence to support the assumption you're making. So, with our example of assuming someone new won't like you because you were bullied in the past, that *alone* isn't the most solid evidence. You have to consider what evidence you have to support that assumption beyond your feelings. You're emotionally reasoning if all your evidence comes back to your emotions—especially if you reject or minimize other facts.

In that situation, you could ask yourself questions such as these to challenge the thought:

- Haven't I also experienced people liking me? Why am I not considering that evidence as part of my reasoning?

- Do I even know why those other people didn't like me? Looking back, is it possible it was because of their trauma or insecurities?
- Isn't occasional rejection part of finding compatible relationships?
- Is my assumption that others won't like me getting in the way of genuinely connecting with people?
- Reflecting on my past experiences of being rejected, if I *unbiasedly* analyze my own behaviors towards those people, did I do something that merited being rejected? Did I engage in behaviors that were harmful to the connection, or were we simply not compatible?
- What areas of growth do I have that could be impacting how my interactions with others go, and what can I do to be mindful of them in the moment while also practicing skills to improve?

When your thoughts come from a rational place, you have evidence to support them beyond emotion. Our emotions provide one piece of evidence, but there will also be others. For example, you feel like a friend is mad at you. If this comes from a place of rational thought, you should be able to identify additional evidence that supports this belief.

Here's what rational thought would look like in that scenario. You think your friend is mad at you (your thought), so you feel hurt (your emotion). They haven't returned your calls or texts (pattern of behavior). The last *couple of times* you tried to make plans, they said they were unavailable (pattern of behavior). In the past, they regularly engaged with your posts on social media, but they haven't over the last few months (pattern of behavior).

Of course, there are still other possible explanations. For instance, maybe your friend is going through a hard time and is struggling to reach out for the help they need. Even with that possibility, assuming they *might* be mad at you is not farfetched. However, jumping the gun and deciding your initial assumption is correct without asking them would be unreasonable. With this scenario, taking the time to thoughtfully point out the pattern of changed behavior and inquire whether they're upset with you would be the most emotionally intelligent thing to do. Asking is your best way to avoid cognitive distortions, like emotional reasoning, and your friend's answer would provide you with the last piece of the puzzle. Too many people have ruined relationships by making false assumptions, and you want to avoid doing that as much as possible.

Sure, sometimes, going with your initial theory may be the best course of action. If your partner has a history of lying and cheating, and you find condoms hidden in their car, it would likely be in your best interest to just trust your gut, given the person's history. But concluding that a friend you've enjoyed a good relationship with is mad at you without even asking them would be unreasonable, even though *thinking* they may be angry at you, considering all the evidence you have, would be a rational hypothesis. Just like in science experiments, having a hypothesis is a sign that you need to investigate further before forming a conclusion. In this type of situation, you don't want to draw conclusions based only on your emotional assumptions. Doing so would increase your likelihood of making a mistake that could damage the relationship.

Avoid getting in your own way simply because you're experiencing heavy emotions like anxiety or fear. It's perfectly okay to be anxious. But you want to do two things: 1) feel what you feel and 2) talk yourself through it in a healthy way that doesn't create a negative self-fulfilling prophecy. Again, there are many times when your emotional reactions genuinely reflect reality, but there are also times when they don't. The problem isn't your emotions but the irrational thoughts your feelings are sometimes based upon. Be willing to analyze situations beyond what you feel, and accept that your thoughts can occasionally be misleading. It's the imperfect nature of being human. When the *specific* situation at hand calls for it (because, again, not all situations will), the goal is to be a good investigator who forms relatively reasonable conclusions by seeking as much information as possible, communicating well with others, and asking follow-up questions.

We all occasionally have irrational thoughts. If you don't identify them as such, you'll have an emotional response that isn't entirely based on reality. But if you recognize an irrational thought for what it is, you'll have a completely different emotional experience.

I firmly believe in trusting intuition, but it is important not to label every emotional experience you have as your intuition because it's not. Most of your emotional experiences are just regular feelings based on thoughts and assumptions you made. Intuition often feels like an inner knowing that goes beyond regular human emotion and can even feel like a spiritual experience. Many people refer to it as a message of clarity that they feel they received from a source. It can also happen in response to engaging in meditative practices or experiencing a strongly detailed, vivid dream that aligns with something happening in the person's present life. Strengthening your relationship with yourself (and being highly mindful of your biases) can help you decipher between your day-to-day feelings and your inner knowing. Even if you believe it is your intuition, it is still essential to determine whether it is necessary to gather additional information before making a decision or taking action. If you decide not to, just make sure that your response to the situation is still a rational and healthy response that aligns with your becoming.

It's important to note that not all intrusive thoughts will call for the rabbit hole method. Again, you can usually dismiss intrusive thoughts that don't feel personal; however, those that feel more personal may not always pass as quickly. The rabbit hole method is meant to help you with the intrusive thoughts that feel harder to move past or have happened repeatedly. Thankfully, most of your intrusive thoughts won't require this much attention, but for the ones that do, remember to give yourself grace and fill the hole.

Little t, Big T

As we've seen, self-awareness and self-curiosity are our best friends. We must be self-reflective if we want to process our experiences effectively. An essential part of doing that and avoiding emotional reasoning is understanding the difference between "little t" and "Big T." You may have heard about the two types of Ts when it comes to trauma, but that's not what I'm referring to here. With my clients, I like to use "little t vs. Big T" to help them better understand their lived experiences.

Little t refers to your experience (your "truth"), and Big T refers to your shared reality with others (your shared "Truth"). Both Ts matter, but it's crucial that you learn to tell them apart because they don't always match. For instance, you might think you're unattractive (little t), but that doesn't mean people won't be attracted to you (Big T). Even if you feel unattractive, some people will still find you attractive because that whole "beauty is in the eye of the beholder" concept is factual. Deep attraction is a complex experience based on many factors, not just looks. We all have differences regarding who we are attracted to, and attraction can also grow between people over time.

Acknowledging the difference between the two Ts helps you avoid getting in your own way. Feeling unattractive (little t) is a real experience you're having. It's causing actual unpleasant feelings for you. Of course, the hope is for you to see your beauty, but in the meantime, the pain of feeling unattractive is real. When you separate your reality (little t) from the reality you share with others (Big T), you can better process and understand your experiences.

As you can imagine, in most cases, Big T tends to be more nuanced and complex than little t. That's because your shared reality with others is rarely black-and-white. Your shared reality tends to be pretty gray because the truths of the world tend to be pretty gray, given that there are 8 billion people in it. Just as we discussed earlier about absolute language, there are very few things that are true *all of the time.*

In this example, the complexity of Big T would include the following facts:

There are billions of people in the world. As of 2023, there are over 250 million adults in the United States alone.

Some of those people will be attracted to you.
- For those attracted to you, the spectrum of that attraction will vary on a scale of slightly attracted to highly attracted.
- Some people will want to date you because of that attraction, and others won't for various reasons, some about you (i.e., personality differences) and others not about you (i.e., they don't want a relationship).
- *You* won't be attracted to or interested in some of the people who are attracted to you, so their attraction to you will matter a lot less.

Some of those people won't be attracted to you.
- Some people who aren't attracted to you can become attracted to you over time after getting to know you.
- Some people aren't attracted to you because of their sexual orientation or other factors that make you incompatible.

These facts are only the tip of the iceberg, so it shows how complex Big T, the shared truth, can be—especially when Big T involves a shared reality with multiple people (i.e., saying *no one* could ever find you attractive, a statement that includes billions of people and is too simplistic to be true). Words matter a lot, especially the ones you say to yourself, so you have to choose them wisely. What you choose to frequently say to yourself will, over time, condition certain beliefs that will affect how you see and experience reality.

A good rule of thumb to avoid emotional reasoning with Big T statements is to assess whether your claims are too simplistic to account for the number of people you're making the claims about. More people means more complexity and variability, so oversimplified claims are often highly inaccurate. In other words, the more people who are part of the shared reality you're making claims about, the more complicated things become. For example, saying a specific person doesn't find you attractive is less complex because it's a shared reality between you and one person. Because of this, it's a lot easier to summarize Big T. Of course, it's important to ask and not assume the person isn't interested in you. That would be the only way to know for sure that the little t (your belief that they aren't interested in you) and the Big T (how they actually feel about you) match.

Since little t is only based on your feelings and experiences, it tends to be a lot less nuanced and more easily defined in most cases. Of course, there will be times when little t and Big T *do* match. You may believe you hurt someone's feelings (little t) and later find out that you did (Big T) by asking them. However, by remaining aware that they don't *always* match, you can better understand and respond to your emotions and experiences.

Seek additional information to avoid emotional reasoning when you realize little t and Big T may not match. One of the best ways to do that is to ask questions. If you think you hurt someone's feelings, asking is the best way to know. If you believe you made a mistake at work, asking would allow you to figure out if you did. Effective, assertive communication is vital, and simply choosing to ask questions can save you from the heartache assumptions often cause. Questions can also help you better navigate your experiences and maintain self-awareness.

Sure, you can do your part by asking questions, and the person you ask can still choose to be dishonest, but thankfully, there are usually other signs. If you feel like someone is being dishonest with you, such as when their story doesn't add up or you have evidence that contradicts what they're telling you, further conversation can help confirm this. Of course, this isn't a foolproof method of figuring out the truth, but if you continue to seek information and things still seem suspicious, it could be a sign that they're being dishonest. It is essential to check your biases and try to be reasonable by considering other explanations without giving too much benefit of the doubt; it's a delicate balance.

When all else fails, remember behavioral patterns can show you the truth that someone isn't willing to say. This is often the most foolproof and reliable way to determine the truth. Our behaviors give off clear, non-verbal messages. If a person says they respect you, but their behaviors tell a different story, believe their behaviors! If you notice concerning behavioral patterns, listen to their behaviors, not their words. (The key word here is "patterns." You don't want to jump to conclusions prematurely). Words are easy to say, but behaviors are hard to consistently fake. When you notice a pattern, point it out in a thoughtful, assertive manner and see how they respond. Do they take accountability? Do they intentionally work on changing this behavior over time?

If someone is genuinely working on themselves, you can see it through changed behavior, accountability, and commitment. Change is not a perfect journey, so mistakes and old behaviors are part of the learning process, but real change yields gradual progress of some kind. Words with no sincere actions create a toxic cycle. They can also be manipulative, such as when a person "changes" for a little while and then goes back to the same behaviors, sometimes with no acknowledgment or accountability.

Your job is to be an effective communicator by bringing the problem to the person's attention—and to listen when someone points out your pattern of behavior. (It goes both ways, but beware of abusive "feedback," like gaslighting and projecting). If you've clearly and consistently communicated an issue to someone, analyzing their behaviors over time can help you see the truth. Remember: you can't change anyone but yourself, and people only change if they want to and are willing to do the work. Plus, a person can want change but also not be willing to do what it takes to create change, so this still will lead to a toxic cycle; our desires don't always match our efforts. To change, we have to have the want *and* willingness. Always be mindful of your behavioral patterns (for your growth and self-awareness) and the patterns of others (for your protection and so you can identify healthy relationships).

Lastly, there are situations where you should just listen to your gut and not seek additional information. Sometimes, following your instinct and emotion is your wisest decision. For instance, when there's a possible *immediate* threat, your feelings are enough justification to remove yourself. Emotional reasoning *is* the smartest thing to do if you feel you may be in danger. If you're walking home late at night and feel you might be in danger, don't stop to get more information. Just run! So what if you feel or look silly? It's better to be safe than sorry. However, in other day-to-day moments, remember to distinguish between little t and Big T.

Magnifying and Minimizing

Another cognitive distortion we've all experienced is magnifying our mistakes and minimizing our achievements. For many of us, this is a learned behavior or trauma response. I initially formed this habit in response to a toxic friendship I had for many years with a person who often made me feel bad about positive things in my life. This friendship started in early childhood and continued until my mid-twenties when I finally decided to end the relationship.

No matter how much I minimized my joy, this person would accuse me of being braggy or full of myself when I shared anything I was pleased or excited about. Over time, this impacted my self-esteem, and I felt like I was doing something wrong by talking about positive things in my life. However, they constantly shared whatever they wanted about their life, good or bad, and I was supportive.

This person often made me feel guilty for celebrating good things, but they were always open to focusing on my mistakes and hardships. They minimized the good and magnified the bad in my life and encouraged me to do the same. Because of this friendship trauma, I did this to myself over the years without even realizing it. When I shared my achievements or anything I was excited about, it made me uncomfortable. I often minimized my good news with everyone because this now ex-friend frequently made me feel like my happiness was an annoyance.

Once I ended the relationship, I had to break this habit and relearn how to share my joy without feeling like I was doing something wrong. I did this by changing my self-talk and holding myself accountable to sharing things about my life, good and bad, with trusted people. I regularly reminded myself that sharing my joy is an entirely appropriate thing to do. I developed new friendships with healthier people, allowing me to get the corrective experiences I needed to heal from the conditioning the former friendship had caused. I once again opened myself to receiving what I was constantly giving to other people: an open, safe space to share whatever they desired. I relearned that I deserved the same in return. I accepted that true friends are happy for your success and don't find joy in your pain.

Regardless of how you may have possibly formed this habit yourself, if you find yourself minimizing your joy and emphasizing your pain, it's vital to break this pattern. Magnifying and minimizing are cognitive distortions. Your victories deserve celebration, no matter how small you think they are. Your mistakes are learning opportunities and should not be used to crucify yourself, even as you take accountability and responsibility for your actions. If you allow yourself to learn from your past and celebrate your achievements, you'll continue to evolve and grow. Mistakes are inevitable, but so are your successes. Be mindful of how you speak to yourself about both, and let self-growth be the goal.

Catastrophizing

With catastrophizing, a type of magnification, you assume the worst will happen even with little to no evidence. Expecting to fail a test even though you studied for a week or always thinking something terrible will happen when your life is going well are examples of catastrophizing. We've already covered how powerful negative thinking can be, so it's clear how this can lead to poor outcomes (i.e., your thoughts can subconsciously impact your behaviors, creating negative self-fulfilling prophecies). But that's not where the problems with catastrophizing end.

When you constantly assume the worst, you frequently find yourself in states of avoidable emotional distress. You unintentionally spend a lot of your energy tending to emotions brought on by situations only happening in your mind, which is not the best use of your energy. Catastrophizing causes you to live a life focused more on your (well-intentioned) false predictions than reality. It can also lead to other biases that cause you distress, like confirmation bias (only accepting information that confirms what you already believe). When done often and especially when not corrected, it creates one big mentally toxic loop.

Moreover, when you don't realize you're doing this, you often fail to properly internalize (process) when the worst *doesn't* happen, leading to more catastrophizing beliefs in the future. Remember: when you don't properly internalize corrective experiences, you cannot truly benefit from them or use them to help shift your mindset going forward. In other words, you struggle to take what you could learn from your experiences to improve your thought patterns, which causes you to stay stuck in the toxic habit of catastrophizing.

Here's what the cycle typically looks like in stages.

Stage #1: You have anxiety about a situation and automatically assume the worst will happen.

Stage #2: You spend a significant amount of time and energy worrying about the worst occurring instead of focusing on ways you could respond to the situation. You're problem-focused instead of response-focused. You also begin to *feel* helpless because not enough of your energy is being focused on identifying actionable solutions.

Stage #3: As time goes on, because you fear the worst-case scenario so much, you fail to reinforce your thoughts about what is *most likely* to happen, which, if done, would actually help you manage your anxiety. Remember: your chosen thoughts are your best defense against the thoughts you don't choose, and whatever thoughts you choose to nurture the most will affect you the most. In other words, when you breathe more life into the catastrophizing thoughts, they end up taking all your mental focus and energy. As time passes, you unintentionally stop entertaining other possible outcomes.

Stage #4: Because so much of your emotional energy is spent entertaining the catastrophizing thoughts, over time, the worst-case scenario begins to *feel* like the most likely scenario, even though, in many cases, it's not.

Stage #5: Later, when the worst doesn't happen, you feel relieved, but because of the time spent catastrophizing about the situation, you end up focusing on whatever didn't go right instead of the fact that the worst didn't occur. You felt sure the worst would happen, so the discomfort of being wrong causes you to continue focusing on the negative even though, deep down, you wanted to be incorrect since, in this case, being wrong is a good thing.

Sometimes, investing your emotional energy in an effort, such as all the time spent worrying and feeling anxious about one possible outcome, can cause you to continue focusing on the negative. You don't want to feel like all the emotional energy you invested was for nothing, so you subconsciously choose to magnify the bad over the good as a way to feel justified about how your energy was spent. In psychology, this is known as the sunk-cost fallacy, which is when a person is unwilling to give up on an approach or perspective even once it is clear that a different approach or mindset would be better, all because they have invested a lot of time, energy or money into it. It's like when you lose a lot of money at the casino, and you keep gambling because you've already "invested" so much. You convince yourself that continuing to gamble will somehow make the money you spent worth it, but in reality, you are just losing more money. Likewise, when you choose to continue to focus on the negative even after everything has worked out, you also continue to lose.

When you invest energy in something, it can sometimes be hard to accept that what you put in is not leading to what you expected, so you try to find other ways to justify your investment instead of admitting that you were wrong. In other words, even when your prediction about the worst happening is incorrect, you may feel compelled to magnify something negative about the situation so the time you spent worrying doesn't feel like a lost investment.

Catastrophizing can sometimes become "addictive" because this five-stage cycle makes it *seem* like thinking this way is the best way to protect yourself when, in actuality, it just makes life ten times harder. Your fear of the worst can quickly turn into believing it will occur because the more you think about it, the more real it feels. But in many situations, the worst doesn't happen, so the energy cost and emotional toll aren't worth it.

In reality, the worst-case scenario rarely occurs, which is why catastrophized thoughts are considered irrational and distorted. If you take a moment to think about it, you'll realize that's true. Sure, bad things happen sometimes, but how often does the *worst*-case scenario happen? Be careful not to label all unfortunate or undesirable outcomes as the worst-case scenario. Most often, these outcomes are inconvenient and maybe even distressing to some degree, but that's not the same as the worst thing that could've happened—self-talk and word choice matter greatly since your thoughts impact your emotions and behaviors. Perspective is everything, so if you choose to refer to every bad thing that happens as the worst, you consequently affect your feelings and behaviors accordingly.

If the worst thing does happen, please acknowledge it as such, but to deal with other worries and fears, ask yourself some of the following critical thinking questions:

- What are you worried about, and how likely is it that this worry will come true?
- What evidence, including past experiences, do you have to support this worry, and are you *reasonably* weighing this evidence? (Be aware of your biases.)
- Are there any other explanations for those past experiences, like unintentional self-fulfilling prophecies?
- If you've experienced similar things in the past, how did you handle the situation, and what can you do differently this time?
- How would you respond to the worst-case scenario if it did happen?
- What are alternative outcomes, and how would you manage those?
- Even if your worries come true, what are the chances that you'll recover and be okay with time?
- If needed, what could you do to seek support from others as you recover?

I covered a few common thought errors, but there are others. The main thing is to be mindful that, as a human, you are susceptible to irrational thoughts. Because of this reality, you have a responsibility to be self-aware and self-reflective, especially since the foundation for your feelings and actions is your thoughts.

Be curious about your thoughts, and be sure to analyze them; attempt to uncover why you have chosen a particular perspective in a specific situation. Practicing this habit is an essential part of self-growth. You don't want to mistakenly believe you're always right or can't improve your mindset.

We all have room to grow, we all have irrational thoughts, and we all have a responsibility to be mindful of the operations of our minds. The best way to lessen how often irrational thoughts occur is to educate yourself on what they are and how they play out in situations. Now that you have this information, your responsibility going forward is to hold yourself accountable for applying it.

Before you knew what an elephant was, you couldn't identify one, right? When you have a label for and a deep understanding of something, you can point it out when you see it or when it happens. Learning the language and how to identify thought errors is the first step to identifying opportunities to correct them. You'll never be able to stop irrational thoughts for good because they're part of your humanity (so that would be an impossible goal to meet). Still, you can practice responding to them better and, through correction, ultimately prevent them from negatively affecting your life. Expect to have them because you will, but no longer allow them to go unnoticed or, worse, uncorrected.

Again, our job isn't to try to become less human because we can't. Instead, our job is to get better at managing our humanness and improving how we move through our human moments. By holding yourself accountable to improving your responses instead of trying to stop the irrational thoughts altogether, you'll find that with practice and over time, they begin to happen less as your skills strengthen and your mindset gets healthier.

Accept that irrational thoughts will happen occasionally and try not to make a big deal when they do. Accept that they're an inevitable part of the human journey, and your job is to learn how to manage them better. Be on the lookout for the ones I covered in this chapter and seek outside knowledge to educate yourself on the many others. When you find yourself having these thoughts, be sure to reflect, shift your perspective when needed, and respond with healthy intentions.

CHAPTER 9

Discovering the Real You

*Your true identity lies within you; all you have to do is
be willing to explore and recondition yourself.*

W e all began life being told what to believe before we even
had a chance to form beliefs of our own. Many of our
parents' beliefs are just *their* parents' beliefs, and if no
one questions what they were taught, the same views can be recycled
for generations despite the existence of new information.

Unless you had parents who encouraged self-exploration, your
opinions about topics like religion, politics, career, and who you are
as a person may not be genuinely yours. They might *feel* like yours
because you were conditioned to believe these things from birth, but
that's not the same as forming beliefs with an open, curious mind.

Close-mindedness doesn't allow us to grow the way open-
mindedness does. Our understanding of the world is constantly changing due to advancements in science, biology, technology, psychology,
and other fields, so we should expect our beliefs to evolve as well. Just

like many of the beliefs from hundreds of years ago are now deemed outdated, inaccurate, and even harmful, we should expect the same to be true about some of our current beliefs. It would be unreasonable to assume we know all there is to know about ourselves, other people, and the universe. Take a moment to think about how unrealistic that assumption would be.

We are all complex, unique individuals, and the universe is possibly infinite. Hell, our earliest ancestors date back 6 million years, and modern humans have existed for 300,000 years. Yet, we've still only managed to explore five percent of the ocean and the universe! We're *far* from fully understanding ourselves as humans, the wonders of the planet we live on, and the universe as a whole.

You were born a whole person, meant to go on a lifelong journey of self-discovery to uncover what's already there within you. You were meant to discover these things free of other's expectations because they're things only you could truly know about yourself. They come from within you and are uncovered through genuine exploration of self and life experiences. However, when you're *conditioned* to believe parts of your authentic self aren't acceptable, this derails you from your life's purpose of self-discovery, and you begin to deny parts of yourself.

We see this in the shaming of a little boy who loves sewing and hairstyling or a little girl who loves trucks and wants to be a construction worker. A person's *true* interests are a product of their self-exploration, individuality, and self-expression, but certain types of conditioning can disrupt this. Adults often discourage certain natural interests because it does not fit the narrow boxes they were *told* to place *all* people in based on their sex chromosomes. Even the media is constantly perpetuating this by conditioning people to believe there are only limited options on who they can become and what they are capable of doing based on that one factor.

Endless research has consistently shown that this can significantly disrupt a child's journey to an authentic life and contributes to many people feeling life dissatisfaction and depression. There are even correlations between lower authenticity and a higher risk for aggressive behavior. [27] Shaming children for exploring their genuine interests has led to many adults pursuing goals based on their conditioning instead of looking within to find goals that align with who they truly are. So many of us are too busy trying to be who everyone else expects us to be instead of taking the time to engage in self-exploration to discover what we enjoy and what we desire for our lives.

One of the most heartbreaking parts of this is that there is no way to know how many people would have accomplished so much more in their lifetime and how that would have positively benefited humanity if they were genuinely doing things they were passionate about. There are probably so many lawyers who were meant to be phenomenal musicians, garbage collectors who would be unbelievably talented designers, business professionals who would love being a head librarian, and medical doctors who would be excellent teachers. We would still have humans in all of these careers (because there are so many of us), but the difference would be that they would also be happier and fulfilled living in their purpose. More people would have jobs that actually match their interests and that bring them the most joy. Their careers would genuinely be their choice based on what they have gotten to know about themselves on their life's journey. I imagine that this would also lead to us having better experiences when interacting and working with people in these roles because they would enjoy what they do and likely, as a result, would be better at it. (And of course, yes, we would need to make it so that all jobs provided a livable wage so this wouldn't be a deterrent, but maybe if people, from birth, were encouraged to pursue their passion according to their authentic selves, this would lead to better lawmakers and outcomes that benefit us all).

From birth, people placed so many expectations on you that had the potential to disrupt your self-discovery. If you were genetically assigned female (XX), you were expected (and even conditioned) to like makeup and dolls. If you were genetically assigned male (XY), you were expected (and even conditioned) to like the color blue and sports. And if you were genetically assigned intersex (XXY, XO, XYY, XXXY—yes, there are more than two possible sex chromosome outcomes), you were treated as an outcast because you couldn't easily be placed into one of the two boxes. [28] These expectations were placed on you despite the fact that there is no reliable evidence that a person's favorite color or toy has anything to do with their chromosomes.

The problem is humans are *way* more complex than their assigned sex at birth. Yes, this is *one* piece of information, but it doesn't tell us much about the unique individual who was just born into the world; only they can tell us who they are, and they can't even speak yet to do so. Our sex alone doesn't determine our natural interests, the perfect career for us, activities we will enjoy, who we are attracted to, our favorite foods, or our unique self-expression; only our individual, open-minded self-exploration can reveal those things to us over our lifetime. Plus, scientifically, we know that many of these things are at least partially (if not more) determined by biological factors that are set *before* we even exit the womb; we are *not* born a blank slate. We are born an individual, and harmful conditioning can strip us of that individuality instead of helping us add to it. Again, this is why it's called self-discovery: we are searching for answers that lie within us, and not doing so is literally living a life at war with your real self.

Who an individual *truly* is cannot be assumed or solely defined by *one* piece of information that tells us very little about their actual individuality, and for so long, we have been conditioning generation after generation to believe otherwise. This conditioning has shaped our world, causing people to mistakenly believe that the patterns we see from the conditioning are due to biological differences when, in actuality, *it is due to the conditioning itself!*

If we are telling and modeling to children that they have to be a certain way or like certain things to be accepted in society, this directly influences their behaviors because, as we have learned, beliefs are just that powerful! Plus, because they are new here, they have no frame of reference to know any better. Any part of their true self that doesn't fit that narrow mold will be more likely to be abandoned or denied, especially if they are frequently teased or ridiculed for an interest they have. They don't yet have a strong sense of self because that takes time to develop and must be encouraged, so this makes them more vulnerable.

We have mistakenly watered down the uniqueness of each human by conditioning people to fall into these black-and-white categories the moment they take their first breath outside the womb and before they even have self-awareness or life experiences. Taking what should have been a colorful world with even more beautiful diversity, self-expression, and individuality and turning it into a world filled with people who have been *programmed* to believe that they were meant to be replicas of others who share the same sex or gender as they do.

The irony is that this pattern of conditioning people based on our expectations of what they should like or who they should be is part of a generational cycle of the same being done to us. We begin to gravitate toward interests *expected* of us instead of ones we *naturally* feel drawn to, making it harder for us to identify who we actually are and what we genuinely like. We become what we have been told is acceptable instead of perpetually evolving more into our true selves and learning about ourselves through our experiences.

As children, we were all naturally driven toward interests that were part of our authentic nature. For instance, so far, my two-year-old is curious about how things work (especially the garage door), and he also loves ducks, so we nurture these interests. Even if they don't turn into something more (because they might not), they're still natural curiosities he currently has independent of our expectations, and they should be honored because failing to do so would be disruptive to his self-discovery journey.

Not everything we gravitate towards as a child will manifest into a part of our life's purpose. However, the point is that many of these things will ultimately be a meaningful part of our self-discovery, so it's important not to have this process unnecessarily disrupted. My son's strong curiosity for how things work may be the foundation for his desire to become an engineer one day, or his love of ducks may be the start of a promising career as a veterinarian. If neither occurs, that's more than okay, but as parents, we will know that it was due to him learning more about himself and not because of us pressuring him to be someone he is not.

When I was eight years old, I discovered I had a strong interest in human development, emotion, and behavior. Thankfully, my mother, without disruption, allowed me to nurture and explore this interest (even though this wasn't the career she initially hoped I would have, and if it had been the 1700s, she probably would have discouraged this interest because girls, especially Black ones, "couldn't" be doctors then). Her willingness to listen to me and accept me as my authentic self is a significant part of why I am a clinical psychologist today. She allowed *me* to tell her who I am. She never tried to condition me to have particular interests; she always encouraged me to be an open-minded, free thinker who curiously explored and questioned things. I am now living in my purpose because she didn't allow her assumptions of who I would be to stop me from becoming who I actually am. Today, she is incredibly proud of what I've accomplished by living authentically and who I am perpetually becoming as I continue to do so. Also, her acceptance of me is why I have discovered many of my own beliefs that differ significantly from hers. Her approach to parenting is the foundational reason why I was able to become my own person; I continuously find sources of genuine happiness in my life, and I confidently know how to think for myself.

Maybe you wanted to be an artist when you were younger, but your parents convinced you to pursue a medical degree. Experiences like this cause a person to look to other people for validation of self instead of looking within themselves and analyzing what they learn about themselves from their experiences. The problem is no one has ever been or will ever be you, so they cannot tell you who you are; they can only choose to *properly* support and celebrate with you as you discover parts of your authentic self throughout your life's journey.

One of the biggest mistakes we make as humans is trying to force each other into boxes, conditioning ourselves to believe there's only one way to be when we're all meant to be very different and authentically ourselves. Parents are supposed to teach us skills to be good humans (social skills) and to help us navigate life well as adults (mental health skills), such as healthy communication, empathy, decision-making, effective conflict resolution, compromise, emotional intelligence, and cognitive flexibility. They are also supposed to teach us basic life skills like cooking, cleaning, money management, and how to change the oil in a car.

However, they were never supposed to tell us who we are, dictate our self-expression (within reason of what was age-appropriate since our brains were still developing), or discourage our individuality. Only we can discover these things because the journey is a personal one for each of us, as we are the *only* person who has ever been or will be us. These parts of the self are discovered by looking within, seeking knowledge, and exploring life with a positive, curious mindset. Parents and other people in our lives are meant to support and encourage our self-discovery journey by safely and lovingly guiding us through it while also continuing to explore their own since it's meant to be lifelong. Because of harmful conditioning and stereotypes, humanity has accidentally become one massive self-fulfilling prophecy. Thankfully, things are slowly but surely improving as each generation becomes more educated on the brain and human development, more empathetic, open-minded, emotionally intelligent, and more willing to look within to discover what has always been there.

Cognitive Dissonance

An essential part of figuring out who we are includes discovering our true beliefs. However, having our current beliefs challenged may make us a bit uncomfortable; this feeling is called cognitive dissonance. Most of us don't naturally enjoy this feeling (I know I didn't), so we have to train ourselves to tolerate it and see the value in it.

Having our beliefs challenged can feel uncomfortable, but it can also lead to meaningful growth. When we're unwilling to learn and take in new, trustworthy information, we hinder our development. Our initial instinct may be to get defensive or shut down, but being open-minded allows us to make sure our beliefs are well-founded and they are indeed our own.

Cognitive dissonance is a type of mental discomfort. Sometimes, new information can feel disruptive or even threatening. It's like someone is shaking our brains. Since, as humans, we value and strongly desire to understand things, thinking we may be wrong about something can feel violating. Many of us find peace in assuming our current beliefs are the "right" beliefs and that they represent all there is to know. The idea of needing to evolve constantly can feel daunting if we do not have a positive perspective.

Cognitive dissonance is something we'll experience an endless number of times throughout our lives. We must embrace it and learn how to respond to it appropriately so we don't hinder our growth. Remember, our goal isn't to become less human but, instead, to respond better to our humanity. We must condition ourselves to view our life's journey and the evolution of our understanding as an exciting reality. Doing so will help us maintain an open mind. It will allow us to develop more accurate beliefs over time because we won't unintentionally shut down information we should actually be considering.

Desiring to stay the same doesn't allow you to get all you can from this lifetime. However, being inquisitive and explorative does.

Why would you ever choose to stay the same when you could use the gift of life to become new and better versions of yourself? There is so much that makes you uniquely you, some of which you haven't discovered yet! This also means there are so many parts of yourself that you can further develop if you're willing to work on becoming comfortable with feeling cognitive dissonance.

When you're presented with information that goes against what you believe, you need to resolve it. You can do this in a few ways:

1. Update or change your belief to include the latest information.
2. Seek more information in hopes that it will resolve the dissonance without you needing to change your beliefs. (Be mindful of the difference between someone's opinions and information that is based on actual research and credible data – we don't know what someone else's opinion is founded upon. It could simply be their conditioning that they have never critically thought about or questioned).
3. Reject the information altogether, which can sometimes lead to lying to yourself, so you can keep believing what you *want* to believe because that feels easier. Of course, new information sometimes *should be* rejected. It all depends on the credibility of the information.

Depending on the circumstances and quality of the information presented, there will be times when any of the three options are appropriate. This is where your critical thinking skills and open-mindedness matter most. In other words, if you constantly find yourself choosing one of the above options and never considering the others when your beliefs are challenged, you're likely preventing your growth.

When you're faced with new information, as long as it's trustworthy, you owe it to yourself to consider it, explore further, and gather more information. Also, remember to be flexible, as there was a time when humans thought it was unreasonable to believe planes could fly or that ships could float. It's clear by now that, as a human, you're susceptible to error, so thinking you know all there is to know will limit you. In many cases, at the very least, seeking more information is a necessary step, specifically seeking additional information in support of *and* against the stance you're considering. The truth is, no matter how much you wish it were the case, none of us know all the answers to life (and we are all constantly being conditioned), so you need to remain in a state of change if you don't want to hold yourself back from accommodating new insights and facts that we discover.

A highly constructive cognitive change to make in order to live more authentically is one that I have already covered: actively working on shifting how you view being wrong by improving your self-talk. So many of us go straight to the defensive when we should go straight to a place of curiosity (I know I used to be very guilty of this myself before I realized the harm it was causing me and others). Despite what your experiences have conditioned you to feel, being wrong is not a threat. It's inevitable, and it's an opportunity to right the wrong. You will be wrong sometimes, whether about a belief you hold, an assumption you make, or an action you take. It's a part of life you must embrace for your own well-being and personal development so you can become a better manager of self and a better person to others.

People who care more about being right than being well-informed don't reach their full potential and stay stuck in a cycle of the same. When you allow yourself to be open and comfortable with challenges to your beliefs, you allow yourself to keep learning. What do you have to lose? If your beliefs are correct, you should still come to that conclusion after seriously and thoroughly considering an alternative perspective or new, credible information. And if they aren't, you will gain new insights and be able to update your beliefs with *valuable* information that will help you grow as a person. The only way to lose is to constantly reject any new piece of information or perspective that contradicts what you currently believe.

Sometimes, we get defensive because, subconsciously, we already know we might be wrong. There is no shame in being wrong, but there is shame in choosing not to learn better when we have endless opportunities to do so. I have trained myself not to fear being wrong because I understand the value it brings me. I care more about being well-informed than I do about holding on to my current beliefs. I desire to have opinions that are well-founded on facts and to be considerate of multiple points of view because often, the truth of things lies in the "gray." As a matter of fact, I expect many of my views will constantly evolve because I plan to continue seeking knowledge. Of course, there are times when we seriously consider contradicting information and find it isn't useful. In those situations, we do not need to update our mindset, but if we don't at least consider it, how can we be sure we're not missing an opportunity for self-growth?

Whether we like it or not, because of human nature, we have all been conditioned and will continue to be conditioned for the rest of our lives. Ideally, we want our conditioning about the world around us to be based on the most up-to-date facts we currently have and the new ones coming that we have yet to discover. Make sure that the ways you are choosing to go about conditioning yourself are conducive to your growth, and account for the fact that our understanding is meant to change throughout our lives. Also, make sure that the people you allow to influence you are helping you meet this goal as well.

Confirmation Bias

Touched on earlier, confirmation bias is when we only accept information that confirms what we already believe. For instance, if someone has a belief that they are incapable, they'll search for evidence to support that core belief and discount evidence that says otherwise. When something negative happens, they'll use that situation to confirm their belief. They'll say things like: "See, I knew I would fail. I always do! That's why I didn't get that job. Who would want to hire someone like me?" When in reality, the fact that they even got the interview shows they were considered a qualified applicant in the first place. Plus, if there was only one position, all but one qualified interviewee was bound to be disappointed by the outcome. And even if they did get the job, they still might discount their abilities, attributing their success to luck or the desperation of the employer, all because of their core belief that they're incapable.

Confirmation bias causes us to ignore other reasonable aspects of a situation as a way to serve our own beliefs. Depression and anxiety disorders can make us more susceptible to processing our experiences in a biased way (and vice versa). The problem is the more someone subconsciously does this, the more depressed or anxious they become. Thinking this way fuels the disorder, whereas changing their thoughts could help them overcome it. This is why cognitive-behavioral techniques are so successful in treating both conditions.

The most common reason we fall for this cycle of experiencing cognitive dissonance and then trying to resolve it using confirmation bias is that we don't even realize we're doing it. Again, this is why having language and knowledge to describe our thoughts and behaviors is so important. When I first learned about confirmation bias during my undergraduate studies, it helped me increase my self-awareness. I began catching my biases so I could correct the thought patterns and benefit from creating a healthier mindset. Once I was able to label the mental somersaults I was doing, I had control over them and could choose to replace my thoughts whenever needed.

Having a better understanding of how your mind works can help protect you from these mental pitfalls. Let's look at some things to keep in mind to help you resolve moments of cognitive dissonance in a healthy way.

If you need to do mental somersaults to justify a decision, it's likely not the best decision. If it's hard to find a reasonable justification for your choice, you should consider whether a different decision is best. This is especially true if the reasons and past attempts have not led to any improvement or positive outcomes. In the abusive relationship I experienced, I used loving the person and hoping for change as reasons to stay as long as I did. For me, the problem with that decision was that nothing had changed in three years despite my consistent efforts, so at some point, I had to accept my hope for change no longer seemed reasonable.

With hope ruled out, that only left me with love as a reason. Yes, I loved him, but that alone does not make for a healthy relationship. I had to face the reality that we are capable of falling in love with the wrong person. It happens all the time. Love, by itself, is not an indicator that a relationship is right or best for us. Plus, love comes in different quantities and qualities; the way I love my husband now is nothing like the love I had for my ex. The love I shared with my ex felt desperate, unsafe, and often painful because it was a chaotic relationship. The love I share with my husband is a deep, passionate love that feels safe, secure, and exciting because it's healthy. It's a type of love I couldn't have felt with my ex because of the issues present in the relationship and who he was at the time (and who he possibly still is—I don't know and no longer wanted to stick around to find out).

Simply put, healthy relationships are rarely a rollercoaster. They grow and evolve for the better over time, which produces more feelings of calm and safety as time goes on (even with the occasional hiccup here and there). Unhealthy relationships become stagnant and stay the same despite efforts toward growth. Whether it's a romantic relationship, friendship, or a professional relationship, as time goes on, if everyone is doing their part to create positive change, things should become more comfortable and stable. If you are doing the work from the beginning of the relationship, early on is typically the hardest time because you're learning about each other, unlearning unhealthy behaviors, working through trauma together, learning how to communicate well, etc. Of course, there will still be challenging moments, but the growth should be noticeable and relatively consistent.

You cannot grow with someone who isn't doing their part to change for the better, no matter how desperately you want them to, because you only have control over yourself and your growth. Someone's lack of change is about their battle with themselves; you're just caught in the crossfire because you have a relationship with them. Know that sometimes walking away is the right decision, and sometimes it's the only option you have to protect yourself and appropriately respond to the feelings of cognitive dissonance.

Unless you have engaged in open-minded exploration, most of your beliefs are based on what people *told* you to believe. This one can be a hard reality to accept, but doing so can free us to begin thinking for ourselves and living more authentically. We've all been conditioned and socialized. It's not that *all* conditioning is bad because it is an inevitable part of living. However, once we are self-aware enough, we can thankfully begin to think critically about the sources of our conditioning, seek new information for future conditioning, begin reconditioning ourselves in ways that we believe are needed, and remain mindful and selective of the people we allow to influence us going forward.

When we came into the world, we relied on the adults who cared for us to tell us about the world, and they could only share what they currently believed. As children, we didn't know anything different. After all, we had just arrived earthside, so we had no frame of reference. We had no choice but to rely on their beliefs. However, as adults, we're now self-aware enough to choose to form views of our own, but of course, this takes deliberate action and often requires unlearning and healing.

As we know, humans can be very susceptible to biases and errors. This is even truer the more generations we go back because the average person was even less informed about psychology and mental health. Remember: when we don't have the language or knowledge to describe the types of thoughts we have or the behaviors we engage in, it's harder to see the errors in our ways. We can engage in cognitive errors, poor logic, and problematic behaviors without even realizing it. This is why psychoeducation is essential for managing our mental and behavioral health. If we don't understand what we're doing, it's a lot harder to stop it, and even worse, we can continue to justify it!

Because of generational beliefs and practices, generally speaking, many of our parents, grandparents, and ancestors were less self-aware. Mental health was even more stigmatized and ignored when they were growing up. If we take the time to reflect, we can see the negative consequences of ignoring mental health in how much our elders suffered trying to navigate life. Many of our parents don't know how to engage in healthy conflict. They lack communication skills, struggle to take accountability for their actions, don't know how to give genuine apologies, are uncomfortable with their emotions, and are unwilling to talk about their feelings. Many of them also struggle with emotional regulation (often seen with outbursts of anger or violence), have substance abuse issues, and have undiagnosed mental health disorders.

Of course, other generational factors also played a role in how their lives went. Many of our elders lived through horrendous life events, and of course, this also shaped their worldview and impacted specific outcomes in their lives. That being said, we need to ask ourselves what this means for the quality of the beliefs we adopted from them.

When we do not seriously care for ourselves mentally, emotionally, and behaviorally, we face devastating consequences. These three areas make up who we are, so not tending to them negatively impacts our quality of life. We cannot expect to reach our best potential while neglecting to care for the central parts of our existence. With each new generation, we need to be explorative and not mindlessly rely on beliefs others have taught us because we have no idea how those people formed their beliefs. We cannot guarantee the person we got our beliefs from thoroughly examined or even fact-checked them. If their views were just based on what their parents told them, then they passed beliefs on to us that haven't been properly analyzed for decades.

Mindlessly following without doing any of our own investigations is problematic because of human nature. We are gaining more knowledge about the world around us every day, so without intentional scrutiny, we could carry outdated beliefs that not only hold us back as individuals but also hold back humanity as a whole.

History shows us that as people question and challenge traditional beliefs, the world evolves into a safer, more peaceful place for everyone (although we still have a *long* way to go). Ableism, homophobia, racism, transphobia, ageism, and other forms of prejudice are all examples of harmful beliefs that have led to tremendous pain and mistreatment of one another for absolutely no reason other than natural human differences.

We do not have it all figured out, but it is clear that close-mindedness, an unwillingness to learn, and a lack of empathy cause a lot of our problems, so much so that many people refuse to acknowledge the parallels and intersectionality between all this unnecessary hate and disconnection. People keep choosing different reasons to hate one another that are all still rooted in the same mindset of "I don't like you or won't accept who you are because you're different from who I am." We see this with Black people hated for being Black, gay people hated for being gay, and little people mocked for their stature, all things people cannot help, and most wouldn't even if they could because these differences are part of the unique diversity of the human experience! It's simply who they are.

Beliefs that invalidate natural differences in the human experience have made the world an unsafe place for people simply trying to exist peacefully as themselves. We should consider whether holding beliefs that can encourage hate, violence, and disconnection from one another is making the world a better place for everyone. (The answer is no, it's not).

Humbling ourselves enough to recognize we don't know everything and being open to learning is how we grow! We need to care more about being well-educated than we do about being right because, with the little understanding we have thus far about the world, we will inevitably *all* continue to be wrong about some (even many) things. We have to be willing to research new facts, challenge our beliefs, listen to alternative perspectives, learn about other people's experiences, and remain curious about the mysterious world we live in. We evolve when we approach life like a curious scientist. To choose a fixed mindset is to choose to limit ourselves in more ways than one. Never allow yourself to stop learning about the world around you and the people in it.

The main thing to remember is to take a moment to reflect and be open-minded to the information when you experience the feeling of cognitive dissonance. Your beliefs may not change, and that's okay. Not every piece of new information will change your views, nor should it. If it did, that would suggest your beliefs are not well-founded. You shouldn't be that wishy-washy and easily influenced, but you should remain curious nonetheless. Believing you already know all there is to know is naïve. Beliefs, when formed properly, are ever-evolving and the products of deep consideration and exploration.

You have nothing to lose by listening to different perspectives, and often, it will be an opportunity to gain something. Sometimes, a perspective will be useless to you, while other times, it may be eye-opening (if you allow it to be). Analyze what is causing your defensiveness. Is it coming from disliking the idea of being wrong, or is it coming from you having genuine evidence that your perspective is right? Also, what is your perspective based on? Conditioning or exploration? Is the certainty of your beliefs based on longevity or up-to-date facts?

Regardless of your beliefs, before forming an opinion on a topic, do your homework and educate yourself. Otherwise, your opinion will be biased. Because of human nature, you have to remain mindful of not only what you believe but also why you believe it and how you initially formed the belief.

For example, before forming a belief about human sexuality, it would be wise to investigate what researchers have discovered on the subject up to this point, as our understanding has vastly changed over the centuries (i.e., scientific research on the human brain, genetics, and hormones and what they tell us *biologically* about sexuality. Also, what we have learned through studying other mammals' sexual behaviors since humans *are* mammals and part of the animal kingdom). Even if you refused to do that, it would, at the very least, be wise to have open-minded conversations with people different from you to avoid a biased perspective. Remember: confirmation bias happens when you ignore or refuse to seek credible information all because it goes against your current beliefs. When you reject information simply because you don't like that it challenges your beliefs, you can unintentionally do yourself a disservice.

Ultimately, how you approach all this is up to you. You are an individual with free will, and you are the only one in control of your opinions. I hope you'll be mindful of avoiding confirmation bias and any other cognitive errors that can get in the way of your growth. I also hope you'll look at cognitive dissonance differently despite the discomfort it can cause.

So much of my growth has come from my openness to challenging my beliefs and facing cognitive dissonance head-on. Doing so doesn't put your beliefs at any risk because new information will either strengthen the current beliefs you hold or shift your beliefs to ones you can be sure are your own because you did your research. Breaking the conditioning is how you become more self-aware and reach a higher consciousness.

I can stand firm in knowing who I am because my beliefs are truly my own, as those yet to come will also be. What I believe today is unrecognizable from what I believed in the past about myself, others, the world, and the universe. The main difference is that I founded my current beliefs upon deep thought, consideration, exploration, and research (instead of my conditioning). They are *my* beliefs, and I am continuously open to expanding upon them until the day I no longer can because I still have more to learn. We all do.

CHAPTER 10

Mindful Words

Words are energy, so they must be used with thoughtful intention.

There is only one person in the universe you can constantly hear, and that one person is you. Even if you wanted to, you could not escape your own voice, and sometimes, you forget to choose your words wisely (it happens to all of us). You might unintentionally get wrapped up in the distress caused by your inner dialogue, so much so that you forget you're in charge of it. Some negative thoughts feel like an ocean wave that sweeps you up, causing you to lose faith in your ability to get yourself back to shore. You hurt because it feels like your brain has betrayed you. In the pain of it all, it's hard to remember just how capable you are and how you can exert control over your mind. This lack of faith in yourself did not grow overnight; it has slowly taken hold over the years. You wonder, "Why am I thinking like this? What's wrong with me?"

I have no way of knowing how long your fight has been, and I understand this may be a big ask, but I need you to start reestablishing faith in yourself. You may be wondering how to do that, and the answer is to choose it. You can make a choice even when you have no faith because choosing is about your free will, not your beliefs. And often, the conscious decision to commit to a choice leads to faith returning over time. Take each moment as it comes, and honor all your progress thus far despite the hardships along the way.

Maybe you've mistakenly chosen to put your confidence in people who were undeserving, but life's gift of free will commands you to reestablish trust in yourself. The most important relationship you have is the one with yourself because it is the foundation for every other relationship in your life, and it determines how well you respond to the experiences you have throughout your life. Look inward and allow yourself to truly get acquainted with what is there. You were born with an unwavering determination to seek the best for yourself, but trauma and people failing to teach you certain skills may have gotten you somewhat off track. Still, the foundation to rebuild trust and connection with self remains within you because you wouldn't be reading self-help books or seeking knowledge if it wasn't there. Your determination for self-betterment shows an unbreakable investment in yourself.

A major part of taking care of your mental health is being sure to put your energy and efforts toward things that are actually in your control; this is where many people go wrong. How you talk to yourself and others is entirely in your control. You are both the puppet and the puppet master and what you choose to hold yourself accountable to and for is totally up to you.

Accept that your brain is going to do things you don't want it to do sometimes, but focus on what you want to do in *response* to those experiences because that's where your control lies. For instance, if something happens and you think, "I am so stupid!" don't just give up because you had that thought. Correct yourself! You haven't failed just because you were momentarily careless with your words. You should expect to do or say things you regret occasionally, but what you do in response to those moments is what matters most.

Perfection cannot be your goal because humanness is imperfection. As you've learned, some of your thoughts are automatic, and all your emotions are, so your initial reaction isn't entirely in your control, but how you follow up is, especially since most of your behaviors are a choice. Part of rebuilding self-faith is a willingness to accept that your expectations of what the journey should be may be stopping you from learning all you can along the way. Remember: perspective is everything, and how you process your mistakes determines what you get out of them. You cannot afford to see them as failures or actions to be excused. You have to accept them as growth areas that you're dedicated to addressing and learning from.

The quality of your self-talk determines how you respond to situations and how well you come to understand them. Dismissing and replacing thoughts is in your control; it is a skill you have to be committed to honing. Each day, ask yourself the two questions I gave you earlier: 1) What would the person I am trying to become think about this situation? and 2) What would the person I am trying to become do in this situation?

Those questions keep you accountable and mindful. Yes, you will make mistakes along the way because we all do, but if you're willing to analyze what occurred, you can learn from it and use that knowledge to benefit your life going forward. When you think back to some of the choices you now regret, many had outcomes you could have reasonably predicted based on early signs if you had slowed down, asked questions, observed patterns of behavior, sought out knowledge, identified parallels to past experiences, processed with safe people in your life, or allowed yourself to accept reality over what you desired things to be.

How many times have you used your self-talk to convince yourself to do things you know you shouldn't or to make excuses for people because you didn't want to accept their patterns of behavior for what they were?

Your problem isn't a lack of wisdom as much as it is stubbornness. You have to choose to hold yourself accountable to seeing your life for what it is if you want to figure out what you can do to get it to where you would like it to be. Your choices can lead to a better life or a worse one, and the quality of your self-talk has the potential to guide you in either direction.

If you want to live a life of continual evolvement, you must be willing to be honest with yourself. No longer running away from your flaws or the flaws of others is how you rebuild trust in yourself. Your expectations of others should align with the messages their behaviors are sending you. You should only update your expectations if their behavioral patterns and choices show evidence of self-work and consistent change. Remain mindful of your own biases and look at their words as secondary to their actions because you will see a person's true intentions and character through their *patterns* of behavior. Also, assessing whether your words tend to match your own actions will help you do the same for yourself, allowing you to identify areas of growth you need to be working on.

The impact your words have on your emotions and behaviors is powerful, so you cannot afford to use your words to convince yourself that your current reality is something it's not, no matter how badly you want that reality to be true. Lying to yourself about someone else's behavior is a form of self-manipulation that prevents you from making good choices and keeps you from remaining aware that something needs to change in order to *create* that different reality. If someone is mistreating you, use the power of your words to accept things for what they are so you can decide what you want to do about it. It isn't your job to try to be their "therapist" and figure out why they are behaving a certain way. Instead, use your energy and self-talk to mentally accept their behavioral choices even if you don't understand them so you can decide what you want to do in response to what is happening.

On the other hand, your expectations of yourself should reflect what's going well and what you need to work on. Again, honesty is key. You cannot use the power of your words to create change when you're being dishonest with yourself but remember to be kind and affirming. There is no need to be cruel with your language, and doing so will only negatively impact your growth journey; we accomplish more change when we don't attack our self-esteem in the process. Use self-fulfilling prophecies to your advantage by saying affirmations and manifestations that align with your goals for yourself (and *choose* behaviors that match). Speak in a way that helps you build self-esteem and in a way that reflects how you desire to feel about yourself. Lovingly tell yourself the things you *need to hear* in order to begin feeling the things you need to feel; this is how you recondition yourself in a positive way over time. Speak life and love into yourself on a daily basis. Even if you don't yet feel or believe what you are saying, choosing to say it anyway is how you begin shifting your beliefs, emotions, and behaviors. After all, the beliefs you currently hold about yourself that are rooted in your trauma are the product of words that someone said to you, and in the beginning, you didn't believe those words either. Yet, because someone continued to say those harmful things to you, unfortunately, you eventually began believing them. Words are indeed that powerful, so imagine what you could accomplish by conditioning yourself with words in a healthy, productive way. Remind yourself that you are capable of change and use your self-talk to encourage a healthier mindset that positively impacts your behavioral patterns.

Change is a steady and gradual process brought on by ongoing commitment. We all have an important choice of deciding how we will use the time and energy we have been given. How are you choosing to spend yours? If you strive for perfection, you will constantly feel like you're failing. However, if you strive for progress in all forms and sizes, you will transform in unimaginable ways. What small changes could you begin making to create progress over time?

The many years of neglecting our mental health have caused us to become careless with words. We mistakenly believe they're no big deal, and people often downplay their significance. However, our words have an undeniable impact on us because they are a primary part of our conditioning, so being intentional in our use of them should be one of our highest priorities. Their power is not in the words themselves but in the meaning we attach to them and how they are delivered. We shouldn't use them recklessly, and whenever we slip up, we should stop, correct, and replace those words with intention. Again, perfection isn't our goal, but correction should be. We should speak in a way that is mindful of the impact our *chosen* words will have and honor them for the power and influence they can have on ourselves and others.

Here are a few examples of how powerful our words truly are. Words can do all this and much more:

- Cause life-changing trauma through psychological and emotional abuse
- Create deep feelings of belonging, love, and affection
- Harm and lower someone's self-esteem
- Help a person heal, unlearn, and recover from their trauma
- Lead to major mental health concerns like depression, anxiety, and suicidal thoughts
- Give people a way to set boundaries to improve their quality of life

These examples, plus more, show us that our word choice shouldn't be taken lightly. Language, because of the significance and meaning of specific terms, is a *powerful* force that can and will alter us and anyone we speak to. The impact our *chosen* words have can literally alter a person's emotional state, change how we see the world, help us rebuild ourselves, or cause someone else trauma. The outcome is largely dependent on our thoughtfulness, intention, honesty, and willingness to respect the energy behind what we allow ourselves to say.

I want you to think to yourself right now that you are a purple unicorn. Were you able to think that thought? Are you able to say those words easily? Of course you are! It's undeniable that, despite the thoughts we don't choose (automatic or intrusive thoughts), we still have the power to choose what we think or don't think, as well as what we say or don't say. When you deny this fact, you relinquish control over the power your words have. You also give up the power you have to change things for the better.

You have to realize and accept that choosing words, in itself, is a simple task. It's easy to overcomplicate it because you mistake your automatic thoughts for your chosen ones, but they are not the same thing. You also may mistake how it *feels* as a reflection of how hard it is, but our emotions and actions are separate things (despite their relationship) because of our free will. Just like you *choose* to go to work all the time, even when you don't *feel* like it. When you separate emotion from it, the behavior of choosing thoughts and words wisely is fairly simple, even if emotionally it feels challenging because of past experiences. Mentally separating the two is imperative for reconditioning. Of course, honor how it feels and tend to those emotions, but also remind yourself that the feeling is separate from the choice. If you can effortlessly say to yourself, "I am a purple unicorn," you can choose to say something you actually need to hear as well. It is a straightforward task with many benefits, so adopt that mindset and practice it daily to improve this skill. There's so much at stake, including your mental, emotional, and physical well-being.

Things to Keep in Mind

Take a moment to ask yourself if there's a better way to express yourself. Your first reaction is not always your best response. We have to remember that we are animals first, humans second, and our higher conscious self third, so we have to assess where our initial reaction is coming from when we are triggered. Some situations require you to take time to process before you address the issue so that you have time to move successfully through these three parts of self. Being mindful of this helps you improve your emotional regulation, communication, and behavioral skills.

If you are particularly affected by an experience, that is a sign that you need to first process what occurred before communicating to those who were involved. Failing to take adequate time to process with yourself and trusted others will put you at a higher risk of poorly expressing yourself. Too often, people make the mistake of reacting instead of responding. When something emotionally triggers us, that is a sign to slow down and process for as long as needed before addressing the situation. This also allows you to gain clarity on your feelings and thoughts so you can communicate them well at a later time.

When you recognize that you could have managed a situation better, choose to learn from that experience. We all have things we need to work on. There's no shame in that. What is shameful is choosing not to work toward change when we see the problem. Also, whenever the situation requires and allows it, attempt to go back and have another conversation. Correcting yourself is a crucial part of growth. You don't want to have a mentality of "Welp! I messed up, and there's nothing I can do about it." Remember always to respect people's boundaries first, but if they're open to it, have a follow-up conversation, sincerely apologize by taking full accountability for your actions, and express what you've learned from the situation without making excuses. The more you practice a skill, the better you get at it.

Assertive communication is a skill you need to practice. Assertiveness allows you to stand up for your needs and wants while still considering others. You're neither passive nor aggressive. Instead, you're thoughtful, direct, and straightforward.

Here are some examples of assertive communication:
- "I've been overwhelmed lately from taking care of the chores. I know you've been busy, but I need your help. Can we make a plan to address this issue together?"
- "No, I won't be able to help you today. I'm taking the day to rest. I might be available to help on Friday. I'll let you know."
- "I know you need to practice singing today, but I also need to study. Would you mind going to a different part of the house so we can both focus on what we need to do?"

Here are some ways to practice assertiveness:
- Be clear about your wants and needs.
- Maintain eye contact. It's okay to look away, but holding some eye contact models confidence and security.
- Listen to the other person without interrupting, and ask them to do the same for you.
- Speak at a reasonable volume. Speaking too softly can come off as passive, and speaking too loudly can come off as aggressive.
- Be mindful of your body language. Have a confident, non-threatening stance.
- Remember to respect yourself. Your feelings, wants, and needs are as important as anyone else's. Express yourself and be respectful to others.
- Use the time *before* addressing the situation to process and work through some of the intensity of your emotions (regulation). When you are processing with your safe people, that is the appropriate time to get cursing, screaming, and other cathartic forms of communication out so you can communicate in a healthier way when actually addressing the situation.
- Plan for important conversations. Think of words you want to use to improve your delivery. Significant discussions are

best carried out once the appropriate amount of time has been taken to prepare for them.

- Once you are ready to address the situation, express yourself in a direct, authentic, productive, and thoughtful manner. If you yell or threaten, you can accidentally take away from your message. "I" statements are a great way to accomplish the goal of being emotionally congruent and productive (sentences that begin with "I" instead of beginning with "you").

"No" is not a bad word. You cannot make everyone happy all the time, and that's okay. Saying no is a way you respect and take care of yourself, especially when you refrain from lying about the reason for your no. No is an answer all on its own, and you don't have to justify it. You can, but it's also okay if you don't want to explain why you are saying no. Either way, don't lie as an alternative because doing so can condition you to believe that meeting your needs is a bad thing. If you want to get comfortable with saying no and not seeing it as negative, you have to practice owning the no yourself. If you are acting like saying no is a bad thing, then you will begin to believe it is a bad thing. As long as your delivery is thoughtful, saying no is an entirely appropriate response to a question or request.

Some people may be disappointed or even angry, but that doesn't mean you did anything wrong. Remember, emotions are produced automatically, and the particular emotions a person experiences in response to hearing no will partially depend on their past experiences. If a person was conditioned to see no as an insult, that doesn't mean it is then your responsibility to manage their triggers; that is something they need to commit to working on and healing from. They are responsible for how they choose to respond to their emotions and thoughts, just like you have the same responsibility. It is important not to normalize people-pleasing behavior; all humans have the right to care for their needs and to be respected. We must model this in order to shift the dynamics of our relationships.

When you respectfully say no to others, you also get to see how much they respect your right to care for your own needs. This reveals their level of emotional maturity and empathy skills. People pleasing makes us susceptible to being taken advantage of, and it increases the risk of forming relationships with others who do not respect you as an individual. You are more likely to attract people who only view others as objects to meet their needs and who expect you to constantly sacrifice yourself in order to have a relationship with them.

Healthy relationship dynamics do involve occasional self-sacrifice, but this should be done based on a person's free choice and desire to give care to the other party, not out of fear of losing the relationship, coercion, or because of an unresolved trauma response like people pleasing. Self-sacrifice should only be done when it is not going to harm the person doing it. If we do not have the mental or emotional energy at the time, self-sacrifice may not be the appropriate choice. You can offer up other solutions or alternative ways for the person to get their need met. If you are open to it, you can also offer a different time when you believe you will be able to help them with their request, but that is a choice you get to make based on the circumstances. We have to care for ourselves in order to even have the energy to care for others without it causing us psychological harm. Healthy relationships involve compromise, patience, and empathy and positively benefit all parties as much as humanly possible.

Boundaries are a necessary part of healthy relationships. You set boundaries because you value the relationship and want to improve the dynamic. When you neglect problems, resentment can grow. The longer you ignore issues, the worse they typically become. Remember: your actions set the tone for your relationships. When followed, boundaries allow your relationships to thrive and help everyone get the respect they deserve.

Have more emotional conversations with trusted people.
Unfortunately, finding people with high emotional intelligence is
still challenging. Thankfully, things are continuing to improve since
more people than ever talk openly about mental health, and this is
leading to increased emotional intelligence. Still, all the years of being
encouraged to suppress have deprived so many people of developing
the skills needed to hold emotional space for others. Few of us were
taught how to have emotional conversations, and many of us feel
uncomfortable having them.

Here are a few guidelines for having emotional conversations. Let's
use the example of someone sharing with you that they're having a
hard day and aren't sure why. Begin by acknowledging the person's
emotions and vulnerability. You can simply say what you observe
about their emotional state. Then, paraphrase what you heard them
say. Lastly, ask if they are open to talking more about it.

That would look something like this: *I am so sorry today has been
challenging. I can imagine feeling this way is frustrating. I'm here for
you. It sounds like you're maybe feeling sad or hurt? If you'd like to, I'm
open to talking more about it. Maybe we can figure it out together.*

By asking permission before diving into more conversation, you
show that you respect their boundaries, which creates a safe space. If
they decline to talk about it, let them know you are open to conversing
whenever they are ready. Also, remind them that talking about our
feelings helps us feel better!

If the person agrees to talk more about it, explore their emotions
with them. Ask them processing questions like these:

- Has anything upsetting or new happened lately?
- When did you notice this change in mood?
- Has anything been on your mind that could be contributing
to these feelings?
- Have you ever felt this way before?

Ask them what they need or how you can support them going forward (if that is something you are open to doing). You don't have to be. That's your choice, and you should also check in with yourself to make sure you have the emotional energy to support them through the situation. If what they share suggests a problem they need help solving, ask them if they're open to suggestions.

Take the time to share your thoughts and feelings as well. Let this person know how you feel about their situation and show them empathy, not sympathy (compassion and understanding, not pity). This helps the person feel less alone and more understood by you, which feels very comforting during times of distress. Empathy allows you to tap into yourself emotionally and imagine what the person must be feeling. In other words, you align yourself with them emotionally and sit with them in those feelings.

Sympathy should be avoided. Empathy helps people feel supported and less alone, whereas sympathy can sometimes make a person feel judged. Sympathy is just feeling sorry for a person and their misfortune. That's not necessarily a bad thing, but when someone is distressed, empathy feels a lot better. It allows you to take things deeper by feeling *with* the person instead of just *for* the person.

Here are a few examples of empathy statements:

- I can see how difficult this has been for you.
- It's normal to feel that way.
- The whole thing sounds so discouraging.
- Things are tough right now, but I'm here.
- I wish I had been there with you when that happened.
- It makes me so mad just hearing about it.
- What you're saying makes so much sense to me.

Additionally, it's okay to bring up personal examples of how you can relate to their situation, *but* this should be brief and summarized.

When someone needs you to hold emotional space for them, you do not want to talk endlessly about yourself or your problems. Saying something like "I can relate to this" or "I've had a similar experience" is enough, and you can provide additional details if the person asks. They may want to hear more about your related experience, but allow it to be their decision.

Holding emotional space in healthy relationships goes both ways, so there will be plenty of times when we can share what we are going through. When the person is trying to share what they are going through, it isn't an appropriate time for us to talk about ourselves incessantly; also, someone frequently doing this to you is equally inappropriate.

Expand your vocabulary. The more words you know, the better you can express yourself! There are simple ways to grow your vocabulary. When you hear an unfamiliar word, look up the definition and try to use the word sometime that week. Fitting the word into your life soon after allows the definition to stick. It helps you add it to your memory and your vocabulary. If the word doesn't naturally come up in conversation, don't forget you can use it as part of your self-talk. When you engage in self-talk, fit the new word in, even if you're just doing it to remind yourself of the definition. Repetition and reminding yourself of the word's relevance helps you remember.

Find fitting labels for your emotional experiences. Find words that accurately express how you're feeling. For example, saying "I'm sad" when you feel disappointed isn't completely accurate. If you need help with emotional language, emotion wheels are super helpful. You can find one you like online with a quick Google search. Print it out and keep it where you can easily reference it when needed. When you add to your emotional vocabulary, you can better understand your experiences, which helps you improve your ability to respond to your needs.

Don't forget to journal. Journaling, especially freewriting, is a great way to uncover your feelings. Doing it regularly allows you to unpack your emotions and avoid bottling them up. Write in a journal to improve your emotional processing and increase self-awareness.

When you struggle to label your emotions, this is sometimes a sign that you haven't processed enough. Processing can be done through freewriting, but it can be done verbally too; I highly recommend both methods. Processing happens when you speak freely about what occurred, which helps you uncover how you feel about it. Don't censor yourself, as this often takes away from the processing experience. Processing is not always linear, so you must allow your thoughts to go where they go, as this helps you tap into your subconscious mind. You can process on your own and with people you trust; for significant emotional experiences, it's important to do both.

Sharing with the right person can help you dig deeper and get more from the processing experience. It allows you to receive alternative perspectives and, when needed, to be constructively challenged. After all, everyone has blind spots and defenses. Processing with another person can help you problem-solve situations if that's your goal. Most importantly, it allows you to have your thoughts and feelings reflected to you, which provides opportunities for further self-analysis.

Humor is great but not always appropriate. One of the most common ways people deflect from their feelings is through humor. Laughter is one of the many joys of life. However, it's all about balance. If you constantly joke about your feelings, you can't appropriately respond to them. Yes, it's okay to joke sometimes, but be sure this isn't all you do. Process and own what you feel. Healing comes from seriously addressing your pain. If you constantly downplay it, you cannot work through it.

Be selective and intentional with your words. That old saying, "It's not what we say but how we say it," is true. Most of the time, the issue is our delivery, not the message. Remaining mindful of your delivery can help you avoid creating more problems. Ask yourself how you would want someone to deliver that message to you and use that as a guide. No matter the message, there's always a way to be thoughtful and honest in your delivery; one without the other is never as good as the combination of the two.

But remember, even if you have the best delivery, it may not be well received if a person has lower self-awareness, especially of their triggers and trauma responses. You have to unbiasedly analyze your delivery *and* someone's response, if you want to determine when and where things may have gone wrong. Sometimes, we can do an excellent job of communicating in a healthy way and still be met with an unreasonable reaction or response from the person receiving the message. Suppose you thoroughly analyze your delivery, check your own biases, and process the other person's feedback with empathy and an open mind. If, after all that, you're still genuinely struggling to see why it was taken so poorly, more than likely, the answer lies within the person receiving the message and not in the delivery itself.

There is always something to be learned from our experiences, so be sure to remain open to constructive criticism that comes from someone who is currently capable of giving rational feedback. If you reflect on the interaction and determine that you didn't make any major mistakes with your delivery, still see if there are any little notes you can take from the interaction to strengthen your communication skills even further and benefit you (and others) going forward.

Remember always to be considerate of other people's feelings and your own. If you are telling someone something disappointing, expect that they will feel disappointed; this is normal and pretty much guaranteed. It doesn't mean you made a mistake as long as your delivery was empathetic and considerate of the fact that you would be delivering possibly disappointing news. We should expect that people will have emotions in response to the things we say and do *because they will*. After all, we are emotional creatures, and our brains produce emotions automatically.

Depending on the situation, you can often even predict the type of feelings a particular conversation might produce. Be sure to consider this and use it to help guide you in forming the best delivery possible; this is part of increasing your emotional intelligence and improving your empathy skills. Your goal cannot be to stop a person from having feelings about what you are saying because they will, and no matter how great your delivery is, you do not control that. We are always in some type of emotional state, and we will always have some kind of emotional reaction to our experiences. Instead, the goal is to communicate in a way that is *considerate* of the fact that humans have feelings and to create a safe space for the person to *feel* those feelings after we deliver our message by not dismissing them, downplaying them, or encouraging emotional suppression.

Check whether your inner voice is genuinely your voice or the voice of someone who traumatized you. If you're like most people, your inner voice was corrupted by someone who caused you trauma. This person could be a parent, a friend, a bully, or anyone else who had a significant negative impact on you. Analyze how you currently speak to yourself and see if it reminds you of anyone from your past who hurt you. Sometimes, this happens because of things said to you when you were younger, but it is essential to note it can occur at any time in your life. You can also have internalized the tendency to speak negatively to yourself from being around people who speak to themselves in a very negative way.

As you work through this, coming up with a nickname for this learned voice can help you separate it from your real one. Tell yourself, "That's my mother's voice, not mine." It becomes easier to identify and correct, and doing so allows you to heal and reclaim your voice over time.

From this day forward, commit yourself to being mindful of the meaning behind your words *before* you say them. Doing so is the foundation for your relationship with yourself and others. Such a simple change can lead to so many positive outcomes. Not only will it allow you to better protect your mental health, but it will also positively contribute to the mental health of others.

CHAPTER 11

A New You & A New Us

This is only the beginning of our perpetual becoming.

Writing this book has been a transformative corrective experience for me, and I hope reading it has been the same for you. I chose the title "A New You & A New Us" for the final chapter because it embodies my hopes for Black people, Black communities, and humanity as a whole. The world is currently going through a shift, and more people than ever are choosing to learn about psychology and human development. This has the potential to be transformative for us and, as a result, for future generations. Through this knowledge, we have the opportunity to break generational curses that have plagued families for centuries because people are now *actually* gaining a proper understanding of humans and our needs. This will lead to healthier adults who embody the skills needed to not only respond better to their human experiences but also improve how we treat and interact with one another, helping us gradually create a world designed to care for the emotional and mental needs we all have.

Despite all the in-depth knowledge we have long had about human development, up until this point, most people have been winging it when it comes to raising children. As a result, this has led to mentally and emotionally broken adults trying to put the pieces of themselves back together. This highly preventable pattern has plagued us for so long simply because so many people have been misinformed and conditioned to believe there is no parenting manual. In actuality, the "manual" is understanding human development, human needs, emotions, the brain, and psychology (which includes healthy, effective parenting techniques that have been *consistently* verified through longitudinal research). These are subjects people have studied for almost as long as we have existed and that we know a great deal about.

Successful parenting is the result of educating ourselves on the science of humans. If I wanted to learn how to build airplanes, I would first need an in-depth understanding of the parts, how those parts work together, and what I need to do and teach myself to make sure I build a plane that flies successfully. Parenting is no different.

The education I have received through my own research, my time in school, my time in therapy, and by critically thinking about my experiences has by far been the most valuable information for navigating life and my humanness better and for raising a mentally and emotionally healthy child. We have long had the means to educate ourselves, but one of the biggest mistakes we have made as humans is failing to prioritize and ensure this information is widespread, common knowledge. The fact that we have acted like only therapists need to know about topics like healthy parenting techniques, brain development over the lifespan, the effects of trauma on the brain, emotional intelligence, and other valuable information about what it means to be human is ridiculous! *All* humans need this knowledge, and it shouldn't only be accessible to some. This knowledge is *the guide* to the human experience, so it shouldn't be a privilege. It is a human right.

If we don't want our future to look like our past and present, it begins with each of us making an individual decision to start healing. It begins with each of us choosing to unlearn toxic conditioning, challenging harmful beliefs, continuously educating ourselves, and spreading this knowledge to others. Humanity's change starts with one person learning, taking accountability, and doing self-work; when we grow as people, it benefits everyone we encounter. We all deserve mental wellness, healthy relationships, and opportunities to thrive, but these things are only possible through individual change. We can no longer afford to neglect the one thing that determines *all that we are and will ever be: our mental health.*

Some parts of you may feel like they're currently broken, but they don't have to remain that way. I cannot promise they'll come back together the way you remember them, but that may not be what you need. On this journey, parts of you will be renewed, discovered, reformed, and abandoned, but it all works together for your greatest good. Be open to the process, and most importantly, trust the process for what it is.

The only limits to your growth are the ones you choose to set, so I ask two things of you. First, commit to your self-growth more than you ever have before. If you are already fully committed, challenge yourself to reach new milestones. Each chapter of your life will bring more opportunities for growth and healing, so this is a lifelong commitment and lifestyle.

It's simple. The day you decide to stop trying is the day you get stuck as whoever you are. Whatever you put your time and energy into, you'll improve, so it's up to you to decide what you want to spend them on. Many of us have wasted so much time and energy investing in the wrong things, including things that are out of our control. You have to invest these valuable resources in the one thing that will make all the difference in your life: your relationship with yourself.

Second, as part of your journey, please be sure to acknowledge and honor all the progress you have already made. All your hard work deserves recognition and celebration! Plus, when you discredit your accomplishments, you decrease the likelihood that you'll continue to make progress. You are so complex. Think about everything that makes you uniquely you. Whatever comes to mind doesn't even include the parts of yourself you haven't discovered yet.

Remember: one of the biggest mistakes you can make is to assume you've learned all there is to know about yourself or others, to get stuck in a black-and-white definition of who you are and what you believe. Your authentic self exists somewhere in the gray because that is the only way to account for the nuance of the world and universe. There's an endless amount of information you can learn about yourself and elements to work on within yourself. Because of this, your potential for growth is limitless if you allow it to be. You develop skills as a result of intentional effort and commitment, so why would you ever want to limit how great you can become?

Of course, who you are today is partially due to your experiences thus far. Maybe you've lived through significant trauma. Maybe the *only* coping mechanism you were ever given was prayer. Maybe you were never really taught how to have a healthy relationship with your emotions. Whatever your trauma, I want you to know I genuinely empathize with you; I'm sure your life hasn't always been easy.

As a trauma survivor myself, I understand how challenging healing can be. I am still a work in progress and forever will be. But I've experienced firsthand my transformation thus far, so I also know that tremendous change and growth are possible. I know how choosing to shift your mindset can remove a lot of the complexity from the journey. This is why I choose to look at life as a series of choices with mostly predictable outcomes if I am well-informed about the decisions I make and take the proper time to process. This is why I am consciously committed to being intentional with my words, both to myself and others. This is why I choose to feel my feelings and learn about what they communicate to me, which helps me better navigate my life and take care of myself. This is also why I actively reflect on my behaviors before I act to make sure they align with my personal development goals—all these commitments to self ensure I am positively *conditioning* myself toward growth, not stagnancy.

Be willing to accept that progress is not linear or perfect; mistakes will happen. Change is about taking gradual steps that add up over time and propel you forward to who you want to become.

Simply put, I hope you allow yourself to do all you can in your lifetime to *heal and thrive.* Since we have all been and will continue to be conditioned, I hope, with the constant access you have to yourself, you choose to condition yourself through self-talk to see life in its simplest form and empower yourself to make the decisions you need to make. I hope you remain open to seeking knowledge that can help you better understand yourself and the world around you. I hope you accept that your emotions do not make you weak; they make you human, and being deeply acquainted with them is a central part of mental wellness.

How many times have you come across a life-changing message, but with time, you allowed it to fade? Too often, we receive lessons but forget to implement them. Choose to apply what you learned in this book, as well as any other valuable information you come across or seek out. Conditioning takes time; you have to practice the skills you want to get better at and remind yourself of the knowledge those skills are based on until it sticks. Knowledge without intentional application is wasted wisdom; don't settle for that because you deserve to use your free will to create the best life for yourself and the best relationship with yourself. You just have to accept that you can't take everyone with you or hold on to parts of yourself that are getting in the way of your progress.

Despite how you may have been conditioned to see things, the truth is you have *never* been incapable. The problem was you were missing the knowledge that would allow you to put your capabilities to the best use and, because of trauma, you were conditioned to disconnect from yourself mentally and emotionally. Self-awareness and psychology allow you to know why you do what you choose to do and help you understand the significance of your experiences with others. The only way to gain a deep sense of inner knowing is to take the time to seek it genuinely. Often, the first step is accepting that you don't know who you are if you haven't yet taken steps to delve within. Running away from your emotions and hard truths, as well as refusing to analyze your thoughts and behaviors, only prevents this understanding from developing. As a result, you won't be able to progressively become a better manager of self. This, of course, impacts how well you navigate your life.

Further, self-growth is not a journey you're meant to go on alone; we all need community. Ironically, being self-sufficient actually requires us to seek help and connection from others. We are able to better care for ourselves when we are willing to accept the help we all need in order to navigate life well. We are all meant to profoundly emotionally support one another by being emotional together. It is up to you to seek relationships with people who are emotionally intelligent and who can propel you forward, not hold you back.

Who you choose to have a relationship with is just that, a choice. Unfortunately, even blood can sometimes be an unhealthy relationship. People can only be as healthy in their relationship with you as they are in their relationship with themselves. Every interaction you have with a person reflects where they are on their mental health journey. No matter how much you wish your interactions with some people could be better, you cannot change anyone but yourself. A person's quality of communication, ability to emotionally regulate, listening skills, ability to perspective-take, and other ways of relating to you all depend on how much self-work they've done up to the current day. In most cases, bad attitudes and behaviors are not a reflection of someone's fixed personality; they are a reflection of someone's current skill set to manage self (or lack thereof)

As humans, we are influenced by the people we surround ourselves with, whether we like it or not, so we *must* be mindful of the company we choose. We should always have empathy and kindness for everyone, and we all need community and connection, so isolation is not the answer. However, having boundaries and severing ties when appropriate are necessary parts of the healing and growth journey.

Yes, it is vital to still interact with others who are in a different place on their journey because people cannot grow without inspiration, new insights, and being lovingly challenged. Plus, we all need to support one another. However, ideally, our *closest* relationships should be with people who are compatible with who we are trying to become. When it is safe to do so, we can and should attempt to inspire others, but we must remain mindful that we cannot change them.

If we hold on to relationships that encourage us to stay the same, it makes it harder to get to where we want to be. This doesn't mean we have to let go of everyone completely; sometimes, all we need is stricter boundaries to create healthy distance. This also helps people understand there are natural consequences to their actions. *Frequent* mistreatment, especially with no *consistent* sign of change and accountability, should eventually lead to the loss of relationships.

When people feel the natural consequences of their actions, this can, over time, lead to self-reflection and even positive change. They begin to realize that how they treat others directly impacts whether they will have those relationships. Change is significantly less likely when we enable others by allowing them to hurt us in the same ways continuously. Our words alone are not enough; we have to change our behaviors and take action in response to their choices.

When you need to let go of someone, you may have to endure some loneliness as you rebuild. Learn to value your own company while putting in the work to improve yourself and find healthier connections. See yourself as a stranger you desire to know as intimately as possible, to be more deeply acquainted with than anyone else. You have that opportunity. Other people get to decide how vulnerable they want to be with you, but you have complete control over how vulnerable you are with yourself. Don't take that for granted. Take full advantage of the level of access you have to yourself. The deeper you dive, the more you will uncover, allowing you to heal, nurture, mature, learn, and unlearn as you continue to grow.

Self-Actualization

You may not be familiar with the term self-actualization, but you may already be living your life in alignment with this concept. The term comes from humanistic psychology. Self-actualization comes from navigating life by concentrating on reaching your full potential and becoming everything you're capable of becoming. It is a decision to make this your life's purpose and goal.

Life circumstances can sometimes cause us to lose focus. Many situations can contribute to a person no longer working toward self-actualization, but all those events can simply be summarized as trauma. The good news is that even when someone has lost this motivation, they can get it back through psychological and emotional healing.

If we could somehow ask everyone if they wanted to reach their full potential, I'm pretty confident almost everyone would say, "Yes, of course!" And if we were able to wave a wand to make that their reality, most people would be open to and excited about it. Unfortunately, self-actualization isn't the result of magic. Instead, it takes hard work and lifelong dedication.

I think of self-actualization as an ongoing state of self, not something we check off a to-do list. If we want it, we must strive to reach it throughout our lives. It's not a destination to get to but something we continuously evolve into with endless levels we can achieve. It's about constantly striving to better yourself with every opportunity you get to do so. It's about being open to growth, learning, and healing.

Dr. Abraham Maslow believed it is rare but possible for someone to *completely* self-actualize.[29] He believed humans are born with the drive to do so, and I agree. However, I think the rarity of this achievement has a lot to do with the toxic ways we have conditioned people, including the harmful beliefs we have *chosen* to pass down despite their inaccuracy and clear adverse effects on the human psyche. This includes toxic (performative) masculinity, toxic (performative) femininity, and emotional suppression. This is why I am fighting for change: to help more and more people accept their humanity, find their true selves, and live authentically. This is how we create and live our happiest, most fulfilling lives.

Because of human complexity and the limitless opportunities for self-betterment, I believe we can reach extraordinary levels of self-actualization in specific areas while striving to do the same in others. Self-actualizing is an overall way of living and approaching life. It's about choosing to live a life where you strive to reach personal goals while also remaining dedicated to overall self-betterment, emotional awareness, continuous learning, self-care, self-expression, empathy, and deep, meaningful connection to others. Living this way is life-changing for me, and research shows it has done the same for countless others, so I want to help as many people as possible dedicate themselves to self-actualizing. It is the most powerful and useful way to spend the time we have been given and to get the most out of this lifetime because it is us choosing to live according to our unique life's purpose, forever unfolding more into who we were meant to become in the first place.

Take, for example, a person's creative spirit. Someone who finds a fulfilling way to honor this part of who they are, maybe by becoming an artist or building things (even as a hobby), will feel fulfilled in this area. Of course, maintenance will still be an essential part of staying self-actualized. If they lose touch with their creative outlets, this could take away from their overall life satisfaction and self-fulfillment. The main thing to remember is that the more layers we unfold and achieve, the more fulfilling our lives become.

As you read through the list of self-actualization characteristics, rate where you fall on a scale from 1 to 5 for each, with 5 being highly self-actualized. The ones you score lowest on (3 or lower) represent growth areas that require self-work, and through practice, you can use a lot of what you learned in this book to progress. The ones you score highest on (4 or 5) represent areas in which you are already doing well, so continue to maintain and make improvements as needed in those areas.

1. You accept and celebrate people's differences, especially the differences that are part of their self-actualization journey. (When we make the world less safe for others to engage in self-discovery, we disrupt their journey and our own.)

   ———

2. You effectively solve problems and are skilled at knowledge-based critical thinking.

   ———

3. You treat others with empathy and have a sense of connection to all people.

   ———

4. You have a well-developed sense of creativity (sometimes referred to as a "creative spirit.")

   ———

5. You form and maintain emotionally deep, meaningful relationships.

   ———

6. You feel comfortable alone and enjoy your own company.

   ———

7. You see the value in spontaneity.

   ———

8. You have a sense of purpose and perform regular tasks geared toward that purpose.

   ———

9. You accurately perceive reality as it pertains to yourself and others. (You are aware of and frequently correct your own biases and can identify when you are being irrational.)

_____

10. You value yourself and your needs.

_____

11. You do what's best for you, even when it's difficult or unintentionally hurts others, while also understanding the necessity and value of occasional self-sacrifice.

_____

12. You're dedicated to learning about your true self, and you abandon identities forced on you by other people.

_____

13. You remain open to new information with non-defensiveness, and you see the value in constructive criticism from others.

_____

14. You remain open to new experiences as part of self-exploration.

_____

15. You strive to have a positive impact on the world and other people.

_____

16. You experience frequent moments of profound happiness.

_____

17. You maintain a sense of childlike wonder; you are excited by newness and have an ongoing appreciation for the goodness of life.

_____

18. You get enjoyment and satisfaction out of the present moment.

_____

19. You tend to feel secure and unashamed of who you are (meaning your authentic self, not the conditioning that has been done to you by others).

_____

20. You enjoy learning and actively seeking knowledge; you do not speak about issues prior to researching and educating yourself. You are also committed to remaining up-to-date with that research as new facts are discovered.

_____

21. In your relationships, you do not avoid conversations, and you are skilled at _healthy_ conflict resolution.

_____

This list is not exhaustive, and there are other elements of self-actualization, but this is a great starting place. I encourage you to research more about self-actualization, as this has been and continues to be a well-investigated area of study in the field of psychology. This is a lifelong journey, so no matter how you score on each characteristic, you are not behind. If anything, this self-assessment provides you with clarity about where you are so you can pour into yourself and get to where you want to be.

Here are my hopes for you as you continue your life's journey:

*I hope you choose to make the best decision even
when it doesn't feel good in the moment.*

*I hope you honor your emotions and make
space for them every day of your life.*

*I hope you allow yourself to care more about learning than being right,
remaining open to changing your beliefs as you continue to learn.*

*I hope you invest in building self-love and confidence
through self-talk and similar positive actions.*

*I hope you feel a sense of internal freedom and peace even in
moments when you remember the problems of the world.*

*I hope you accept that no one knows everything and that this
motivates you to keep curiously questioning and seeking knowledge.*

*I hope you live your life truly getting to know yourself for who
you are and not just who others conditioned you to be.*

*I hope you live your life getting to know others for who they are
and that your actions and words support this human endeavor.*

I hope you find and live in your purpose.

*I hope you take the time to seek knowledge that helps you
continuously form your own beliefs instead of just following
the beliefs you were conditioned to have from birth.*

I hope when you don't understand something or someone,
you lead with curiosity, not hate or judgment.

I hope you find joy and reconnect with your childlike wonder.

I hope you choose relationships that serve you
well and help you self-actualize.

I hope you lead with empathy and compassion for yourself and others.

I hope you have meaningful interactions with people who are
different from you so you can see the humanity in everyone.

I hope you allow yourself to get all you can
out of this life and possibly the next.

A New Us

The fact that Black mental health hasn't been prioritized is not, of course, entirely our fault. For centuries, generations of Black people have been stuck in a state of survival, and now many of us are repeating what we learned growing up without much reflection. We have a responsibility to do what we can to reverse these harmful effects, even if only on an individual level.

As I've described, your individual growth leads to collective change through the improved quality of your interactions. Plus, as you grow, you're bound to positively influence and motivate others to do the same. Although you only control your own change, your transformation can be a catalyst for someone else's. After all, a healthier you contributes to healthier generations to come, whether you decide to have kids or not, simply because you are constantly interacting with others.

Your job is just to improve yourself, and those improvements will automatically be experienced by others as you live your life. Whatever an individual decides to learn from their experiences is not in your control, nor is it your responsibility. You should be a model for what's possible, but you cannot do anyone else's self-work for them. You can only give support, provide the knowledge you've acquired, and be a positive influence for those who allow you to be. And when people are unwilling to change, all you can do is be empathetic, provide thoughtful feedback about your interactions with them, set healthy boundaries, and self-reflect on what these interactions reveal about what you can work on to keep growing as a person. We are all on similar but separate journeys, and although we need each other to grow, you cannot force connection.

Here are some facts that show why we need to continue to destigmatize mental health in Black communities:

1. Rates for depression continue to rise for all age groups.[30]
2. Black people frequently experience racism, inequality, police brutality, discrimination, and other forms of oppression. All this can not only be stressful but also traumatizing and can have a profound negative impact on a person's mental health.
3. Black Americans are one of the least likely groups to seek mental health treatment despite rising rates of mental health conditions. Unequal access to healthcare and stigma are two major reasons. [31]
4. There are still many harmful parenting beliefs in Black communities that unintentionally perpetuate generational trauma and increase poor mental health outcomes for Black people.[32]
5. One study showed that 63% of Black people believe a mental health condition is a sign of personal weakness.[33]

That list is by no means exhaustive. Plenty of data indicates the need for a shift in how we discuss and manage mental health in the

Black community (and in the world as a whole). I am by no means asking you to tackle all these issues. So many factors play a role. But since we share a culture, we can continue to normalize mental wellness, therapy, and self-work as staples of Black culture.

Let's speak more about professional careers in mental health because we need more of us! We need more of us, not because it's impossible for therapists of other racial and cultural backgrounds to effectively treat Black people, but because many Black people are very reluctant to open up to therapists who don't look like them. Several Black clients have told me they wouldn't be in therapy if I wasn't Black. Representation matters; having more Black therapists and therapists of color creates an increased willingness to seek therapy and safe spaces to heal.

When we consider all we've been through, historically, presently, and personally, it is clear mental healing is imperative. I want us to do more than just survive; I want us to thrive as a people! Of course, accomplishing this goal will take major changes that will by no means happen overnight. We must overcome multiple societal barriers for this to happen.

We have a broken educational system that negatively impacts people of color and deprives millions of children and adolescents of a quality education. We have a broken judicial system that frequently harasses, murders, and fails Black people and people of color. We have an extremely racially and politically divided country plagued by the constant distribution of fake news and media propaganda as a means to keep us divided. We have colorism and stereotypes born out of White supremacy that have even been adopted by some Black people, which further divides us.

But as we have always done, we continue to make major progress and overcome barriers, especially when we work together to create positive change and support one another. Look at how far we have come since slavery and segregation. There was a time when it was illegal for us to learn how to read or write, and here I am writing a book as a Black doctor! Yes, we still have a lot more work to do, but just like our ancestors, we are capable!

There are many ways to work towards positive change as an individual:

- Support foundations that provide mental health services and fight to decrease stigma.
- Use social media to reach as many people as you can to share knowledge.
- Have conversations that disrupt harmful thinking and behavior; thoughtfully call people out when they say or do something wrong.
- Fight for political change and social justice by voting and peacefully protesting (and also consider running for political positions if that interests you).
- Have more social events at your home with your friends and family that help normalize vulnerability and mental health discussions.
- Create an online group for mental health support and conversation.
- Continue to better yourself and learn about and care for your mental health.
- Normalize seeking help and being vulnerable by doing so with people in your life who have the emotional intelligence to support you the way you deserve. Also, be this person for others.

All this, plus more, can make a massive difference. If we each reach only one person, that can add up to millions of people! You don't have to do it all. Working on you alone will have a significant impact on our communities, so helping others do the same is a bonus!

Of course, your first priority should always be to protect your well-being. Please don't put yourself in toxic situations to try to help someone else. Just like I'm doing with this book, there are many ways to help someone help themselves without getting directly involved. Together, we can continue to grow as people.

I commit to continuing to do my part to contribute to our change. Let's do all we can to lift each other up and end the stigma around mental health. Let's all embrace our humanness for what it is so we can finally learn how to *truly* be human together. Let's undo the wrongs and make a world compatible with human emotions and needs. The world that, deep down, we all desire to live in because if we had properly embraced and learned from our humanity long ago, we wouldn't have chosen to create the current world.

The right world for humans is one where the beauty of diversity is celebrated, connection is abundant, emotional support is endless, resources are bountiful, and curiosity is valued. A world where the skill of empathy is nurtured, crying is normal, and loving affection is freely given. Where preventable trauma *is* prevented because people do the work to educate themselves, listen to one another, and have high self-awareness when it comes to how their actions impact other people. Where a stranger is not someone to fear because, from birth, people get their mental and emotional needs met, so it is safe to interact with new people. Where accountability is taken, sincere apologies are given, changed behavior is frequent, and emotional intelligence is widespread. Where we no longer have robotic expectations for humans and mental healthcare is one of our greatest priorities.

The right world for humans is one where self-expression, individuality, and self-discovery are primary objectives encouraged from birth so people can find and more easily become their authentic selves. Where we understand that an individual must look within to discover who they *already are*. Where it is considered shameful to get in the way of someone's self-discovery. Where we don't condition people to live the life we think is ideal for them, but instead understand that their ideal life is one only they can discover.

A place where people choose to seek adequate knowledge before forming opinions. Where people understand it is a strength to admit when you don't know something because that is where learning, growth, and positive change begin. Where people are open to changing their beliefs because they understand that, as we advance as a species, we are learning new things about humans and the world every day.

We deserve a world where parents actually take the time to educate themselves about the science of human development and healthy parenting techniques; that way, they are genuinely prepared for the job and know what it takes to raise healthy adults. Where asking for help and learning from others are among our highest priorities. Where people don't choose to be parents simply because they think they have to; instead, they do so based on their personal desire and understanding of what the role entails, independent of anyone else's expectations. Where providing deep love and teaching life, as well as social and mental health skills, are the primary focuses of parenting. Where abuse is no longer excused, tolerated, or taught. Where we lead with and model love, patience, understanding, empathy, and humility.

This is the way things were always meant to be based on human design, and for too long, we have allowed toxic conditioning to keep us from creating this reality.

We cannot create this world overnight, but we can choose to be a reflection of this world every day. No action means no change, and no change means more suffering for humankind. Each of us, as individuals, makes up what the world is, and our actions and words reflect what the future will be. *We make the world,* so it is our responsibility to change ourselves so it can change too. Be mindful of how you condition yourself and others. Critically think about the messages you send through your behaviors, as these are often the loudest things we say. Realize the things you are running from inside of you could heal you if you were just willing to connect with self.

Learn what it means to be human and choose to accept your humanness. We need each other to survive, and we are not meant to hold the weight of the human experience alone. The quality of our mental health determines how well we "human" together. We have struggled and suffered long enough. It's time we accept the truth that our history has revealed: *neglecting mental health is how we got here, and prioritizing it is how we will change the world.*

At the foundation of almost every human problem is preventable poor mental health, whether it's the lack of empathy that allows us to let humans live in poverty despite having the resources to change that or the stigma we have created around mental health that stops many from having safe spaces to be a human who feels. These poor outcomes for adults are a result of *preventable* generational trauma, a lack of education, and toxic conditioning (not being taught skills like empathy, how to self-reflect, and emotional intelligence.) Our brain houses who we are, and the quality of the care we provide to it determines our becoming. We have to take care of it; the state of the world and humanity will continue to be at risk if we don't.

You may have reached the end of this book, but this is also a new beginning—a new beginning for you and a new beginning for us. Your daily choices determine who you become, so use the gift of life and knowledge to perpetually evolve into greater versions of yourself. Never stop learning from the lessons your experiences bring. Revisit this book often so you can practice and apply its wisdom to your life.

Things change when you choose to no longer be a sheep and instead emerge as a shepherd who challenges norms that should never have been normalized in the first place—a shepherd who breaks patterns that clearly cause harm and don't work. Become someone who frequently looks within and encourages others to do the same. You must own your story if you want to heal what needs to be healed and identify what needs to be nurtured.

Remember, there is no such thing as being unbothered; every experience has and will shape you. You must live your life aware of this fact so you can make choices that lead to healthier experiences. You are affected and will continue to be, but you get to decide what you will and won't tolerate when it comes to your own behaviors and the behaviors of others. Psychology is your guide to understanding; seek this knowledge often so you can have a foundation through which to process your experiences.

You may not have been given the tools you needed to navigate your human experience well, but you now know how to get them and can instill them with practice, just like you were meant to do in the first place. You were born with purpose, and it is not too late. You are your own project, *Bold. Black. & Becoming,* and you must do daily intentional work to progress. If you choose to use your free will to make the most of this life you have been given by listening, learning, seeking help, and encouraging others to do the same, you *can* thrive. You *will* thrive.

After all, you are and have always been a capable superhero.

Acknowledgments

First and foremost, I would like to thank God, the universe, my ancestors, and my spirit guides, who protect me and guide me through this life each and every day. I remain open to the signs and messages brought my way. I vow to stay connected and to continue to live in my soul's purpose in this lifetime and the next.

Thank you to my husband and forever best friend, Javon. Words cannot express how much you do for me and the way you love me. I am forever grateful for finding and choosing you. You know me better than anyone, and just being with you has been the source of so much healing. Your support throughout the process of writing this book was infinite, and you are a major part of why it exists. You were made for me. I love you, baby.

To my son, Elliott Javon, you are my inspiration. You remind me every day of the beauty of our humanness simply by existing and being authentically you. My greatest goal is to make sure your light always shines brightly in this world and to unconditionally support you as you discover who you already are. Thank you for showing me what it means to be human and for being my greatest teacher. I love you endlessly.

To my mom, Sherrie, and my dad, Asment, who have poured into me since birth and have always believed in me. Thank you both for supporting me and allowing me to discover who I already am.

To my sisters, Alengta and Keisha, and my brother, Lamin, thank you for your ongoing support during the creation of *Bold. Black. & Becoming*. Your words of encouragement and investment in me mean more than you know.

To my best friends, Ashley and Marvin, thank you both for being the best-chosen family a person could ask for. The love and support you have shown me, not just throughout this writing process but for as long as I've known you, are the epitome of true friendship. Also, to my other close friends, you all mean the world to me. I appreciate you cheering me on and believing in me even when I doubted myself. Love you all.

To my editor, Candice, thank you for seeing my vision for *Bold. Black. & Becoming* and for your invaluable insights. I am forever grateful.

Lastly, to all those who have ever supported me and who have played a positive role in my becoming, from the bottom of my heart, thank you.

Appendix

Chapter 1: Why You Should Care & How Psychology Can Help

[1] Alegría, Margarita, Lisa R. Fortuna, Julia Y. Lin, Fran H. Norris, Shan Gao, David T. Takeuchi, James S. Jackson, Patrick E. Shrout, and Anne Valentine. "Prevalence, risk, and correlates of posttraumatic stress disorder across ethnic and racial minority groups in the United States." Medical care 51, no. 12 (2013): 1114-1123.; Archibald, Paul C. "Factors Influencing the Relationship Between Work-Related Stress and Posttraumatic Stress Disorder Among Working Black Adults in the United States." The Yale journal of biology and medicine 94, no. 3 (2021): 383-394.; Bird, Claire M., E. Kate Webb, Andrew T. Schramm, Lucas Torres, Christine Larson, and Terri A. deRoon-Cassini. "Racial discrimination is associated with acute posttraumatic stress symptoms and predicts future posttraumatic stress disorder symptom severity in trauma-exposed Black adults in the United States." Journal of traumatic stress 34, no. 5 (2021): 995-1004.; Jones, Audrey L., Jane Rafferty, Susan D. Cochran, Jamie Abelson, Matthew R. Hanna, and Vickie M. Mays. "Prevalence, Severity and Burden of Post-Traumatic Stress Disorder in Black Men and Women Across the Adult Life Span." Journal of Aging and Health, (2022). https://doi.org/10.1177_08982643221086071.

[2] "AACAP Policy Statement on Increased Suicide among Black Youth in the U.S." 2022. Www.aacap.org. March 2022. https://www.aacap.org/AACAP/Policy_Statements/2022/AACAP_Policy_Statement_Increased_Suicide_Among_Black_Youth_US.aspx.

[3] "Mental and Behavioral Health - African Americans | Office of Minority Health." n.d. Minorityhealth.hhs.gov. https://minorityhealth.hhs.gov/mental-and-behavioral-health-african-americans.

[4] Barnett, Tracey Marie, Ashston McFarland, John W. Miller, Victoria Lowe, and Schnavia Smith Hatcher. "Physical and mental health experiences among African American college students." Social Work in Public Health 34, no. 2 (2019): 145-157.; Brooks, Jasmin R., Robert Joseph Taylor, and Linda M. Chatters. "The impact of traumatic events on mental health among older African American and Black Caribbean adults." Journal of aging and

health 34, no. 3 (2022): 390-400.; Carden, Keisha D., Danielle L. McDuffie, Kaleb Murry, Chuong Bui, and Rebecca S. Allen. "Minority stress process among older Black Americans: the role of age, perceived discrimination, and anxiety." Aging & Mental Health 26, no. 4 (2022): 852-859.; Mental Health America. 2020. "Black and African American Communities and Mental Health." Mental Health America. Mental Health America. 2020. https://www.mhanational.org/issues/black-and-african-american-commun ities-and-mental-health.

    5 Vance, Thomas A. 2019. "Addressing Mental Health in the Black Community." Columbia University Department of Psychiatry. February 8, 2019. https://www.columbiapsychiatry.org/news/addressing-menta l-health-black-community.

    6 Evans, Shani Adia. ""I wanted diversity, but not so much": Middle-class white parents, school choice, and the persistence of anti-black stereotypes." Urban Education 59, no. 3 (2024): 911-940.; Johnson, Abbie-Gayle. "Fake news simulated performance: gazing and performing to reinforce neg-ative destination stereotypes." Tourism Geographies 26, no. 1 (2024): 82-96.; Meacham, Ashley M., Heather M. Kleider-Offutt, and Friederike Funk. "Looking more criminal: It's not so black and white." Memory & Cognition 52, no. 1 (2024): 146-162.; O'Flaherty, Brendan, and Rajiv Sethi. "Stereotypes, crime, and policing." Annual Review of Criminology 7 (2024): 383-401.; Hamilton, Alexus. "Black therapists' experiences with their Black clients: A systematic review." Journal of Marital and Family Therapy 50, no. 1 (2024): 150-174.; Volpe, Vanessa V., Julia M. Ross, Abbey Collins, Briana N. Spivey, Natalie N. Watson-Singleton, Rachel W. Goode, Lori S. Hoggard, and Cheryl L. Woods Giscombé. "Gendered Racial Microaggressions and Emotional Eating for Black Young Adult Women: The Mediating Roles of Superwoman Schema and Self-Compassion." Psychology of Women Quarterly 48, no. 1 (2024): 93-107.; Wilson, Elizabeth J., Anahi R. Primgaard, Erin P. Hambrick, Jacob M. Marszalek, Jannette Berkley-Patton, Johanna E. Nilsson, and Kymberley K. Bennett. "Rumination mediates associations between microaggressions and sleep quality in Black Americans: the toll of racial microstressors." Journal of Behavioral Medicine (2024): 1-16.

    7 Eylem, Ozlem, Leonore De Wit, Annemieke Van Straten, Lena Steubl, Zaneta Melissourgaki, Gözde Topgüloğlu Danışman, Ralph De Vries, Ad JFM Kerkhof, Kamaldeep Bhui, and Pim Cuijpers. "Stigma for common mental disorders in racial minorities and majorities a systematic review and meta-analysis." BMC Public health 20, no. 1 (2020): 1-20.; Harris, Janeé R. Avent, Edward Wahesh, Marah Barrow, and Jessica A. Fripp. "Demographics, stigma, and religious coping and Christian African Americans' help seeking." Counseling and Values 66, no. 1 (2021): 73-91.; Harris, Janeé R. Avent, Loni Crumb, Allison Crowe, and Jasmine Garland McKinney. "African Americans' Perceptions of Mental Illness and Preferences

for Treatment." Journal of Counselor Practice 11, no. 1 (2020).; Turner, Erlanger A., Courtland Douglas, and Abdul Haseeb. "Predictors of seeking mental health treatment in black men: therapy fears and expectations about counseling." Community Mental Health Journal 60, no. 2 (2024): 385-393.; Yu, Yu, Samantha L. Matlin, Cindy A. Crusto, Bronwyn Hunter, and Jacob Kraemer Tebes. "Double stigma and help-seeking barriers among Blacks with a behavioral health disorder." Psychiatric Rehabilitation Journal 45, no. 2 (2022): 183.

[8] Deza, Monica, Johanna Catherine Maclean, and Keisha Solomon. "Local access to mental healthcare and crime." Journal of Urban Economics 129 (2022): 103410.; Graaf, Genevieve, and Lonnie Snowden. "Public health coverage and access to mental health care for youth with complex behavioral healthcare needs." Administration and Policy in Mental Health and Mental Health Services Research 47 (2020): 395-409.; Pugh, Mickeal, Paul B. Perrin, Bruce Rybarczyk, and Joseph Tan. "Racism, mental health, healthcare provider trust, and medication adherence among black patients in safety-net primary care." Journal of clinical psychology in medical settings 28 (2021): 181-190.; Thomeer, Mieke Beth, Myles D. Moody, and Jenjira Yahirun. "Racial and ethnic disparities in mental health and mental health care during the COVID-19 pandemic." Journal of racial and ethnic health disparities 10, no. 2 (2023): 961-976.

[9] Lenoir, Caron. 2024. Review of Why Is It so Hard to Find a Black Therapist? Edited by Jess Barron. Https://Meetmonarch.com/. Monarch. January 30, 2024. https://meetmonarch.com/health-resources/articles/therapy-101/why-is-it-so-hard-to-find-a-black-therapist.; Moore, Carrington, Erica Coates, Ar'Reon Watson, Rebecca de Heer, Alison McLeod, and Arielle Prudhomme. ""It's important to work with people that look like me": black patients' preferences for patient-provider race concordance." Journal of racial and ethnic health disparities 10, no. 5 (2023): 2552-2564.; O'Malley, Lisa. 2021. "Addressing the Lack of Black Mental Health Professionals." INSIGHT into Diversity. November 17, 2021. https://www.insightintodiversity.com/addressing-the-lack-of-black-mental-health-professionals/.

[10] Catale, Clarissa, Silvia Bussone, Luisa Lo Iacono, Maria Teresa Viscomi, Daniela Palacios, Alfonso Troisi, and Valeria Carola. "Exposure to different early-life stress experiences results in differentially altered DNA methylation in the brain and immune system." Neurobiology of stress 13 (2020): 100249.; Holz, Nathalie E., Oksana Berhe, Seda Sacu, Emanuel Schwarz, Jonas Tesarz, Christine M. Heim, and Heike Tost. "Early social adversity, altered brain functional connectivity, and mental health." Biological psychiatry 93, no. 5 (2023): 430-441.; Soares, Sara, Vânia Rocha, Michelle Kelly-Irving, Silvia Stringhini, and Sílvia Fraga. "Adverse childhood events and health biomarkers: a systematic review." Frontiers in public health 9 (2021): 649825.

[11] Colman, Andrew M. 2015. A Dictionary of Psychology. 4th ed. Oxford: Oxford University Press.

Chapter 2: Healing Your Relationship with Yourself

[12] Nelson, Tamara, Naysha N. Shahid, and Esteban V. Cardemil. "Do I really need to go and see somebody? Black women's perceptions of help-seeking for depression." Journal of Black Psychology 46, no. 4 (2020): 263-286.; Thorpe, Shemeka, Candice N. Hargons, Jardin N. Dogan, Shawndaya Thrasher, and Danelle Stevens-Watkins. "Incarcerated Black men's restrictive emotionality: The influence of parental closeness and childhood abuse." Psychology of Men & Masculinities 22, no. 4 (2021): 844.; Weiss, Nicole H., Emmanuel D. Thomas, Melissa R. Schick, Miranda E. Reyes, and Ateka A. Contractor. "Racial and ethnic differences in emotion regulation: A systematic review." Journal of clinical psychology 78, no. 5 (2022): 785-808.

[13] "Changes Psychology." 2017. Changes Child Psychology. July 14, 2017. https://changespsychology.com.au/brain-emotions-behaviours/.; Feldman, Lisa. 2018. How Emotions Are Made: The Secret Life of the Brain. S.L.: Mariner Books.; Ledoux, Joseph. 2008. The Emotional Brain the Mysterious Underpinnings of Emotional Life. Paw Prints.; "Emotion Facts: Emotions in the Brain." n.d. Www.brainframe-Kids.com. https://www.brainframe-kids.com/emotions/facts-brain.htm.

[14] Joel, Daphna. "Male or Female? Brains Are Intersex." Frontiers in Integrative Neuroscience 5, (2011). https://doi.org/10.3389/fnint.2011.00057.; Joel, Daphna, Zohar Berman, Ido Tavor, Nadav Wexler, Olga Gaber, Yaniv Stein, Nisan Shefi et al. "Sex beyond the Genitalia: The Human Brain Mosaic." Proceedings of the National Academy of Sciences 112, no. 50 (2015): 15468-15473. https://doi.org/10.1073/pnas.1509654112.; Ruigrok, Amber N., Gholamreza Salimi-Khorshidi, Meng Lai, Simon Baron-Cohen, Michael V. Lombardo, Roger J. Tait, and John Suckling. "A Meta-analysis of Sex Differences in Human Brain Structure." Neuroscience & Biobehavioral Reviews 39, (2014): 34-50. Accessed March 9, 2023. https://doi.org/10.1016/j.neubiorev.2013.12.004.

[15] Algorani, Emad B., and Vikas Gupta. "Coping mechanisms." In StatPearls [Internet]. StatPearls Publishing, 2023.; Kim, Youngmi, Kyeongmo Kim, Karen G. Chartier, Traci L. Wike, and Shelby E. McDonald. "Adverse childhood experience patterns, major depressive disorder, and substance use disorder in older adults." Aging & Mental Health 25, no. 3 (2021): 484-491.; Vintila, Mona, Otilia Ioana Tudorel, Adelina Stefanut, Alexandra Ivanoff, and Venera Bucur. "Emotional distress and coping strategies in COVID-19 anxiety." Current Psychology 42, no. 20 (2023): 17503-17512.

[16] American Psychological Association. 2012. "Understanding Psychotherapy and How It Works." Apa.org. 2012. https://www.apa.org/

topics/psychotherapy/understanding.; Lindberg, Sara. 2020. "Benefits and Options for Therapy." Healthline, October 24, 2020. https://www.healthline.com/health/benefits-of-therapy.; Olivine, Ashley. 2022. "8 Benefits of Therapy." Verywell Health. March 24, 2022. https://www.verywellhealth.com/benefits-of-therapy-5219732.; Parekh, Ranna, and Lior Givon. 2019. "What Is Psychotherapy?" Www.psychiatry.org. American Psychiatric Association. January 2019. https://www.psychiatry.org/patients-families/psychotherapy#:~:text=About%2075%20percent%20of%20people.

[17] Merriam-Webster. 2022. The Merriam-Webster Dictionary. Merriam-Webster.

Chapter 3: Be Response-Focused

[18] Brown, Danice L., Christopher B. Rosnick, and Daniel J. Segrist. "Internalized racial oppression and higher education values: The mediational role of academic locus of control among college African American men and women." Journal of Black Psychology 43, no. 4 (2017): 358-380.; Kang, Hannah Soo, Kyle Edward Chang, Chuansheng Chen, and Ellen Greenberger. "Locus of control and peer relationships among Caucasian, Hispanic, Asian, and African American adolescents." Journal of Youth and Adolescence 44 (2015): 184-194.; Zahodne, Laura B., Oanh L. Meyer, Eunhee Choi, Michael L. Thomas, Sherry L. Willis, Michael Marsiske, Alden L. Gross, George W. Rebok, and Jeanine M. Parisi. "External locus of control contributes to racial disparities in memory and reasoning training gains in ACTIVE." Psychology and aging 30, no. 3 (2015): 561

[19] "Grief vs. Depression: What You Need to Know and When to Seek Help." n.d. Hospice of the Red River Valley. https://www.hrrv.org/grief-support/grief-vs-depression-need-know-seek-help/.

Chapter 4: Avoid Helplessness

[20] Maier, Steven F., and Martin E. Seligman. "Learned helplessness: theory and evidence." Journal of experimental psychology: general 105, no. 1 (1976): 3.; Nickerson, Charlotte. 2023. "What Is Learned Helplessness and Why Does It Happen?," April. https://www.simplypsychology.org/learned-helplessness.html#:~:text=Martin%20Seligman%20and%20Steven%20F.

Chapter 5: Corrective Experiences

[21] "[2023] the Real Odds of Experiencing a Plane Crash." 2020. April 16, 2020. https://flyfright.com/plane-crash-statistics/#:~:text=You%20would%20need%20to%20board.; "Full Year 2022 U.S. Airline Traffic Data | Bureau of Transportation Statistics." 2023. Www.bts.gov. March 16, 2023. https://www.

bts.gov/newsroom/full-year-2022-us-airline-traffic-data#:~:text=For%20
the%20full%20year%202022.

22 CDC. 2022. "Lightning Strike Victim Data." Centers for Disease
Control and Prevention. September 16, 2022. https://www.cdc.gov/disasters/
lightning/victimdata.html#:~:text=But%20the%20odds%20of%20being.;
"Yes, You Can Survive a Plane Crash: Tips from a Longtime Safety Expert |
Frommer's." n.d. Www.frommers.com. Accessed February 24, 2023. https://
www.frommers.com/tips/airfare/airline-accidents-dont-have-to-be-fatal-ti
ps-for-surviving-an-plane-crash-from-a-safety-expert.

Chapter 6: Trauma Responses

23 Levine, Peter A. 2012. Healing Trauma : A Pioneering Program for
Restoring the Wisdom of Your Body. Lexington, Ky.

24 Bernock, Danielle. 2014. Emerging with Wings. 4f Media.

25 National Institute of Justice. 2016. "Children Exposed to Violence."
National Institute of Justice. September 21, 2016. https://nij.ojp.gov/topics/
articles/children-exposed-violence.

Chapter 7: Self-Fulfilling Prophecies

26 Rosenthal, Robert, and Lenore Jacobson. 1968. "Pygmalion in the
Classroom." American Educational Research Journal 5 (4): 708. https://
doi.org/10.2307/1162010.

Chapter 9: Discovering the Real You

27 Hendel, Hilary Jacobs. It's not always depression: Working the change
triangle to listen to the body, discover core emotions, and connect to your
authentic self. Random House, 2018.; Petersen, Anders. "Authentic self-realization
and depression." International Sociology 26, no. 1 (2011): 5-24.; Pinto, Diana
G., John Maltby, Alex M. Wood, and Liz Day. "A behavioral test of Horney's
linkage between authenticity and aggression: People living authentically are
less-likely to respond aggressively in unfair situations." Personality and Individual
Differences 52, no. 1 (2012): 41-44.; Sexton, Jared Yates. The man they wanted
me to be: Toxic masculinity and a crisis of our own making. Catapult, 2020.;
Sutton, Anna. "Living the good life: A meta-analysis of authenticity, well-being
and engagement." Personality and Individual Differences 153 (2020): 109645.;
Turner, Lisa A., Robert D. Faulk, and Tully Garner. "Helicopter parenting,
authenticity, and depressive symptoms: A mediation model." The Journal of
Genetic Psychology 181, no. 6 (2020): 500-505.

28 Viloria, Hida, and Maria Nieto. 2020. The Spectrum of Sex. Jessica
Kingsley Publishers.; Bainbridge, David. 2009. The X in Sex. Harvard

University Press.; Weingarten, Cynthia N, and Sally E Jefferson. 2009. Sex Chromosomes. Nova Science Pub Incorporated.; "Differences in Sex Development." 2017. Nhs.uk. October 18, 2017. https://www.nhs.uk/conditions/differences-in-sex development/#:~:text=Some%20people%20have%20a%20chromosome.; "X and Y Chromosome Variation Center - the Focus Foundation for X & Y Chromosomal Variations." n.d. The Focus Foundation. https://thefocusfoundation.org/x-y-chromosomal-variations/#:~:text=The%20sub%2Dcategories%20that%20exist.

Chapter 11: A New You & A New Us

[29] Maslow, Abraham. 1943. A Theory of Human Motivation. Lulu. com.; Roy José Decarvalho. 1991. The Growth Hypothesis in Psychology : The Humanistic Psychology of Abraham Maslow and Carl Rogers. San Francisco: Emtext.

[30] Goodwill, Janelle R., Robert Joseph Taylor, and Daphne C. Watkins. "Everyday discrimination, depressive symptoms, and suicide ideation among African American men." Archives of suicide research 25, no. 1 (2021): 74-93.; Malloy, Domonique L. "The effects of negative social media in the depressive symptomology of African American adolescents." PhD diss., The Chicago School of Professional Psychology, 2021.; Skipper, Antonius D., Andrew H. Rose, Noel A. Card, Travis James Moore, Debra Lavender-Bratcher, and Cassandra Chaney. "Relational sanctification, communal coping, and depression among African American couples." Journal of Marital and Family Therapy 49, no. 4 (2023): 899-917.

[31] Abdullah, Tahirah, and Tamara L. Brown. "Diagnostic labeling and mental illness stigma among Black Americans: An experimental vignette study." Stigma and Health 5, no. 1 (2020): 11.; Caraballo, César, Dorothy Massey, Shiwani Mahajan, Yuan Lu, Amarnath R. Annapureddy, Brita Roy, Carley Riley et al. "Racial and ethnic disparities in access to health care among adults in the United States: a 20-year National Health Interview Survey analysis, 1999–2018." MedRxiv (2020).; Silva, Nelma Nunes da, Veronica Batista Cambraia Favacho, Gabriella de Andrade Boska, Emerson da Costa Andrade, Neuri Pires das Merces, and Márcia Aparecida Ferreira de Oliveira. "Access of the black population to health services: integrative review." Revista Brasileira de Enfermagem 73 (2020).; "Understanding Mental Health in Black Communities | McLean Hospital." 2023. Www. mcleanhospital.org. January 30, 2023. https://www.mcleanhospital.org/essential/black-mental-health#:~:text=Statistics%20tell%20us%20that%20about.; Yu, Yu, Samantha L. Matlin, Cindy A. Crusto, Bronwyn Hunter, and Jacob Kraemer Tebes. "Double stigma and help-seeking barriers among Blacks with a behavioral health disorder." Psychiatric Rehabilitation Journal 45, no. 2 (2022): 183.

[32] Avezum, Marina Dias Macedo de Melo, Elisa Rachel Pisani Altafim, and Maria Beatriz Martins Linhares. "Spanking and corporal punishment parenting practices and child development: a systematic review." Trauma, Violence, & Abuse 24, no. 5 (2023): 3094-3111.; Duong, Hue Trong. "Childhood experiences and attitudes toward corporal punishment: the mediating role of perceived efficacy of alternative discipline strategies among low-income Black, Hispanic, and White parents." Journal of interpersonal violence 37, no. 19-20 (2022): NP18266-NP18290.; Lee, Yoona, and Malcolm W. Watson. "Corporal punishment and child aggression: ethnic-level family cohesion as a moderator." Journal of interpersonal violence 35, no. 15-16 (2020): 2687-2710.; Patton, Stacey, Toby Rollo, and Tommy J. Curry. ""The first mark of pain": Toward a child-centered methodological reorientation of social theory, race and corporal punishment in American life." Sociology Compass 15, no. 12 (2021): e12943.; Sta, Ceypatto. "Corporal Punishment Harms." The Legacy of Racism for Children: Psychology, Law, and Public Policy (2020): 35.

[33] National Alliance on Mental Illness. 2020. "Mental Health in African American Communities: Challenges, Resources, Community Voices." NAMI California. 2020. https://namica.org/mental-health-challenges-i n-african-american-communities/.

Made in United States
Orlando, FL
04 September 2024

51106895R00147